Native American
Prayer Trees
of Colorado

Native American
Prayer Trees
of Colorado

John Wesley Anderson

Honoring the Past

Shaping the Future

Circle Star Publishing
Colorado Springs, Colorado

᯽

Published in the United States of America

Circle Star Publishing
P.O. Box 60144
Colorado Springs, Colorado 80960

Native American Prayer Trees of Colorado
Anderson, John Wesley

ISBN 978-1-943829-01-9

Library of Congress Control Number: 2018946766

Publisher's Cataloging-in-Publication Data:

Names: Anderson, John Wesley, author.
Title: Native American prayer trees of Colorado / John Wesley Anderson.
Description: Includes bibliographical references. | Colorado Springs, CO: Circle Star Publishing, an imprint of Rhyolite Press LLC, 2018.
Identifiers: LCCN: 2018946766 | ISBN: 978-1-943829-01-9
Subjects: LCSH Indians of North America--Spiritual life--Colorado. | Ute Indians--Colorado--Antiquities. | Trees--Colorado. | Historic trees--Colorado. | Trees--Symbolic aspects. | Ethnoecology. | BISAC HISTORY / Native American | NATURE / Regional | HISTORY / United States / State & Local / West (AK, CA, CO, HI, ID, MT, NV, UT, WY)
Classification: LCC E99.U8 A53 2018 | DDC 979.004/974576--dc23

᯽

Circle Star Publishing is an imprint of Rhyolite Press LLC
www.rhyolitepress.com
PRINTED IN THE UNITED STATES OF AMERICA
Cover design: Donald Kallaus
Book layout: Susie Schorsch
Photography by John W. Anderson except where noted.

Dedication to the Elders

This book is dedicated to the Elders from more than 500 Native American Indian Tribes that once spread across the vast expanse of the North American continent. Their words of wisdom continue to guide and inspire us today. It is also dedicated to the spirits of the trees that were modified by many Native Americans.

Southern Ute Tribal Elder Dr. James Jefferson, pictured above, teaches about Trailmarker Trees: *"The people who shaped these trees didn't do it for themselves, they knew where they were; they did it for future generations."* (Photograph by Bob Wells used with permission.)

Wisdom of the Elders

"Tell me a fact, and I will learn. Tell me a truth, and I will believe it. But tell me a story, and it will live in my heart forever."
— Native American Proverb

"Every society needs sacred places. A society that cannot remember its past, and honor it, is in peril of losing its soul."
— Vine Deloria Jr., Lakota Scholar

"If the rivers die, we die. If the trees die, we die. If animals die, we die. We live these words. Let us ensure that these words live."
— Chief Tatanka-Iyotanka (aka Sitting Bull) Lakota (Sioux)

"God gave us each a song."
— Ute Proverb

"All things share the same breath – the beast, the tree, the man. The air shares its spirit with all the life it supports."
— Chief Seattle (Si´ahl), Duwamish

"When we show respect for other living things, they show respect for us."
— Arapaho

"You already possess everything necessary to become great."
— Crow

"In every deliberation, we must consider the impact on the seventh generation…even if it requires having skin as thick as the bark of a pine."
— Iroquois Laws from the Iroquois Nation

"If we can't protect the Earth, can't protect the sky, if we can't protect our sacred sites, then we've failed the world."
— Jewell Praying Wolf James, Lummi

Foreword

My name is Dr. James M. Jefferson; I am a Ute Tribal Elder. I was born on September 24, 1933 on the Southern Ute Reservation and am the great-great-grandson of the Ute Chief Severo. I grew up listening to the Elders and Medicine Men of my tribe teach about the cultural traditions of my People. I did not have to read about the culture and traditions of my People; I lived it.

I earned a doctorate degree in linguistics, spent several years at the Smithsonian Institute in Washington, D.C., working to preserve the history of Native American people and coauthored the book *The Southern Ute, A Tribal History*, published by the Southern Ute Tribe, Ignacio, Colorado. I serve and have served on the board of directors for many non-profit organizations, including the Old Spanish Trail Association and the Southern Ute Cultural Center and Museum, working to preserve the history and culture of my People.

I have also worked for the last few years with Dr.s Forrest Ketchin, Gary Ziegler, Lois Adams, Manuel Molles and Mary Anne Nelson, along with many non-degreed researchers and historians, including Don Wells, Celinda Kaelin, David Johnson and John Anderson, to study Culturally Modified Trees (CMT) so that we can better accept peeled bark and arborglyph varieties of CMTs. I can confirm the existence of Prayer Trees that were used by my ancestors for navigational, medicinal, burial, educational and spiritual purposes.

As a Ute Tribal Elder and Spiritual Leader I am restricted on what I can disclose publically, beyond the actual existence of Prayer Trees; however, I have conducted extensive field research on public and private land with the individuals name above and hosted several conferences in El Paso County and meetings on the two Ute Reservations in Colorado to exchange information and share the findings of our research which has been conducted throughout many counties located across present day Colorado.

I have also sought counsel and guidance from Ute Medicine Men, Spiritual Leaders and Tribal Leadership, including Southern Ute Tribal Chairman Clement Frost, although I cannot publicly disclose our sacred tribal traditions or ancient ceremonies involving Ute Prayer Trees, I can confirm they do exist. I make this statement, confirming the existence of Ute Prayer Trees, so that these living Native American artifacts, located on the ancestral homeland of the Ute, along with the memory of my ancestors whose hands shaped these sacred trees, will long endure.

Signed, James M. Jefferson Ph.D.
         January 19, 2017
         Southern Ute Reservation Ignacio, Colorado

Timeline

The Ute People claim they were brought to the Shining Mountains by Creator at the beginning of time. They have no migration story and say, "We have always been here, and we will always be here…." When asked about the discovery of America, Dr. Jefferson replies, "We had a pretty good idea where it was all along."

1 AD Shoshonean speaking peoples separate from other Uto-Aztecan groups.

1276 Anasazi began movement out of the adobe cliff dwellings of present-day Mesa Verde.

1492 Columbus discovers America.

1540 Coronado Expedition launched from Mexico along the Rio Grande into American Southwest.

1580 Ute acquired horses from the Spanish (Ute claim to be the first tribe to adopt the horse culture).

1598 Spanish settled into present-day northern New Mexico and begin to establish trade with the Ute.

1610 The pueblo of Santa Fe is established and serves as the Capital for the Spanish Northern Frontier.

1637 Spanish Governor de Rosa reports the capture of 80 Utacas forcing them to work in the mines.

1657 One El Paso County CMT began to grow pointing to Pikes Peak, confirmed through dendrochronology. Other CMTs around Ute Territory modified even earlier confirmed by size.

1705 Comanche establish a presence in present-day Colorado and learn to modify trees from the Ute.

1746 Spanish defeat combined mounted force of Ute and Comanche warriors north of Abiquiu (NM).

1754 Ute enter into an alliance with the Jicarilla Apache (the two tribes remain loyal to one another).

1776 Fathers Dominguez and Escalante attempt an overland crossing to the Pacific led by two Ute.

1778 Bernardo Miera y Pacheco completes a map detailing Yutas (Ute) and Comanche encampments.

1779 Juan Bautista de Anza soldiers and 200 Ute & Jicarilla Apache defeat Comanche Cuerno Verde.

1803 Napoleon sells Louisiana Territory to United States for $15 million fueling westward expansion.

1806 Zebulon Pike enters eastern boundary of Ute land proclaiming one of the Ute's most sacred sites as "Grand Peak," now known as Pikes Peak.

1820 Cheyenne and Arapaho tribes relocate in Ute territory after being forced out of Black Hills (SD).

1830 Congress passes Indian Removal Act forcing relocation of Native American tribes into the west.

1858 Gold discovered by the Greene Russell Party in Cherry Creek launches Pikes Peak Gold Rush.

1864 Cheyenne and Arapahoe warriors declare war in Colorado (ends 5 years later with their removal).

1876 Colorado becomes 38th state of the United States.

1879 Meeker Massacre results in forced relocation of the last free Ute onto reservation lands.

2018 Formation of the Association for Native American Sacred Trees and Places (NASTaP).

Table of Contents

Acknowledgment and Appreciation

Like my journey studying CMTs, writing a book is a journey taken by not only by the author, but those who insure that the project is completed. I would like to thank my publisher Suzanne Schorsch of the Old Colorado City Historical Society who helped with the research, layout, editing and content of this book and spent numerous hours on this journey, making this book come to fruition. Also a special thanks to Elizabeth Taylor for all her time spent proofing the book.

To my family, especially my wife Brenda and daughter Laynie, I want you both to know how much your enduring love and support has meant to me all these years. I sincerely appreciate your continued understanding of my passion for history and need to tell the epic story of the American west—thank you. For all my extended family and personal friends, especially Dr. James Jefferson, Southern Ute Tribal Elder, and those mentioned in this book who have shared their stories and this journey with me, thank you. Lastly, I would like express my sincere appreciation to my attorney, Steve Bain, who stood by me to ensure that the story of the Native American Prayer Trees of Colorado could be told.

Thank you all!

John Wesley Anderson

The Journey

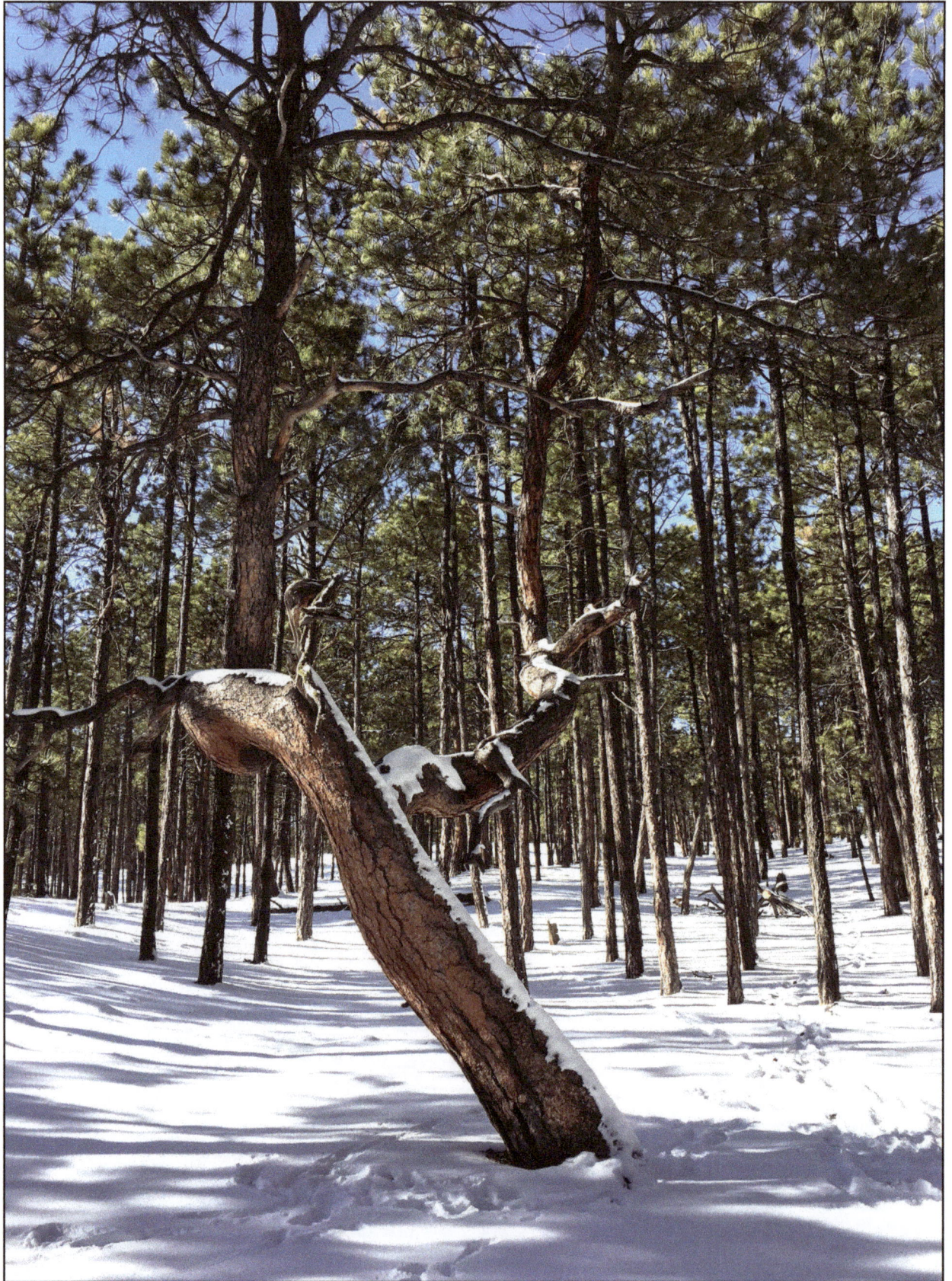

The Journey Continues

The journey I started many years ago, to understand Culturally Modified Trees (CMTs) left behind by Native Americans, especially those created by the Ute whose ancestors lived in Colorado, has been very fulfilling. Along the way I wrote the book *Ute Indian Prayer Trees of the Pikes Peak Region* to interest others in the preservation of these trees. Since publication of that book, my journey continues with many like-minded individuals joining. The passion of others researching CMTs is evidenced by the hundreds of people who have hiked and attended lectures with me, on and off the Ute Reservations. They are active in finding ways to document, photograph and describe CMTs for future study and preservation.

Many before me have also been interested in CMTs. A November, 2016 article in *Landscape Architecture*, "Searching for a Sign" tells of landscape architect Richard Gloede's early efforts to protect "old Indian trail trees" along the shores of Lake Michigan. In 1929 he wrote of over 100 trees that he photographed, measured and located. The trees were those that had been manipulated by indigenous people of the Great Lakes to provide landmarks where others did not exist, trail marker trees. Where forest growth was so thick that it was hard to recognize landmarks, trees were modified to become navigation tools. Gloede felt it was important to save and study the trees as a way to teach about the indigenous people in the region. The article states in the 1920s ordinary citizens were familiar with these historic CMTs, but with the onslaught of the Great Depression, the trees were all but forgotten. Upon the death of Gloede in 1940, questions arose again on the need to properly chart and give special care to these trees.

According to Carl Andrew Koehler's research in the book *Talking Trees & Spirit Trails*, early maps of the United States point out evidence of Native American CMTs. An 1830s map of Northern Michigan labels several sites near Native American villages as "crooked or bent tree trails." There was an Ottawa village called L'Arbre (Crooked Tree) noted in the 1750s.

Today Dennis Downes, who formed the Great Lakes Trail Marker Tree Society, gathers evidence and searches for old journal articles referencing CMTs. Downes acquired Gloede's photographs. One glass plate photograph acquired by Downes shows a tribal leader standing atop a bent tree, smudging stick in hand. Smudging is a ceremony where tobacco or herbs and grasses are lit on fire and the smoke is used to wash over the body to cleanse the body and spirit. The Ute believe that the smoke will carry prayers, made during the ceremony, up to the Creator. Andrew Johnson, the Executive Director of the American Indian Center in Chicago, which represents over 100 tribes, says of Downes: "The Native American Trail Marker Trees are historical links to our past and were a part of the daily lives of many original inhabitants. Our Community is indebted to Dennis Downes for his important and inspiring efforts to discover, properly identify, and preserve these trees throughout the United States. We are honored by his commitment and support his tireless work."

Don Wells, one of the founders of a group called the Mountain Stewards, studies old trails in the Appalachian Mountains and Native American CMTs that mark trails. Don admits that academics are particularly resistant in acknowledging these trees. If fellow Ph.D.s haven't written about these trees, they don't exist, seems to be the attitude of many people of the academic world. The book *Mystery of the Trees*, written by Don and his wife Diane published in 2011, looks at the trail saving efforts of the Indian Trail Mapping Program. This group represents the growing interest in CMTs found in North America. With regard to the existence of CMTs, well known dendrochronologist, Dr. Henri Grissino-Mayer, from the University of Tennessee, wrote to Don Wells: "…no natural disturbance process in forest (such as ice storms, wildfires, insect outbreaks) causes this particular resulting tree form. In other words, I really do not think these are freaks of nature, I have to think that these trees were indeed crooked on purpose, by humans."

Renewed interest in CMTs in both the United States and Canada can only advance the understanding of the Native Americans who modified trees. The article in *Landscape Architecture* magazine points out that "to determine whether a tree is a historic marker or simply an accident in nature is a complex and messy process." Being difficult and messy has not deterred those of us in the Rocky Mountains who want to understand and learn from these historic trees and the culture of the Ute People.

This book will highlight some of these fascinating trees, the journey and stories that have taken us to the trees and look back in time to learn about the indigenous people and other Native American tribes who once inhabited Colorado.

The Ute

The Ute believe that all things made by the hands of the Creator have a spirit. The bear, an eagle, a person or a tree, all have a spirit and at the end of life, Mother Earth reclaims physically what is hers. The spirit will ascend to the Creator to spend eternity. This book is the story about Prayer Trees, also called Spirit Trees by some Ute Elders, found in the Rocky Mountain Region and the people behind these sacred trees, primarily the Ute.

The ancient Ute referred to themselves at the Nuche, The People; however, other Native American tribes knew them as the Mountain People. The homeland of the Ute extended from today's northern

New Mexico, across Colorado to Wyoming and from the eastern plains of Colorado west across the Rocky Mountains into Utah (a state named after the Ute). The Ute's annual migration routes led them in the spring from their lower winter encampments up into the higher elevations in summer, completing a circle. According to Ute Tribal Elder Dr. Jefferson, the Ute generally travelled in a counter clockwise direction, from the lower elevations to higher, and then back to winter at lower altitudes. Dr. Jefferson's Ph.D. is in linguistics. He worked for the Smithsonian Institute in Washington, D.C. preserving the history of Native American people and has become my mentor, helping me understand the culture of the Ute people.

It remains a mystery when the Ute first arrived in the Shining Mountains, their name for the Rocky Mountains, or even from where they came. The Ute do not have a traditional migration story, such as crossing over the Bering Land Bridge that connected North America with Asia during the last Ice Age some 13,000 years ago, as other Native American Tribes believe. The Ute do claim DNA evidence establishes a Ute presence in the Rocky Mountains 14,000 years ago; however, the Ute's Creation Story teaches them that the Creator brought them to the mountains at the beginning of time from the Pleiades, the Seven Sisters, the nearest star cluster to planet earth.

It was the Spanish who documented first contact with the Ute, as the Spanish Conquistadors explored South and North America to search for gold and spread the word of God. The Spanish Conquistadors traced the Rio Grande and the Colorado River to their headwaters, high into the Rocky Mountains. Early Spanish maps drawn during the 1500s show their northern frontier with a horizontal line across the top, north of Santa Fe and Taos, with arrows pointing up and journal notations in Spanish "Here live the Yutahs."

The Spanish first attempted to enslave the Ute, as they had done with other indigenous people of South America, but soon learned it was best to keep peace with the Ute, and eventually they became loyal trading partners. In 1776, two Spanish priests, Father Dominguez and Father Escalante, set out from Santa Fe to establish a trade route to the West Coast. Ute scouts helped guide them across much of what became known as the Old Spanish Trail. By 1779 continuous raids by the fearsome Comanche, who had become known as the Lords of the Plains, disrupted the balance of trade between the Spanish and Ute until the Governor of the Spanish northern frontier, Juan Bautista de Anza, aligned 600 of his soldiers with 200 Ute and Jicarilla Apache to hunt down and kill the fierce Comanche War Chief, Cuerno Verde (Green Horn).

There were many tribes that traveled the Rocky Mountains. The Cheyenne and Arapahoe had a presence in Colorado but did not arrive until the early 1800s and left within a lifetime. There is no historical record that tribes that lived on the Great Plains had a tradition of modifying trees.

The Comanche and Cherokee do have a history of modifying trees but a consistently sustained presence in the area belongs to the Ute. We are not saying that the Ute were the only ones that could have modified trees in the Rocky Mountains, but they certainly had the earliest and the most sustained presence with an oral history that teaches tree modification traditions.

Many of the roads we travel today throughout Colorado's Rocky Mountains follow old Indian trails; a few still lined with Ute Trailmarker Trees. As I continue to research CMTs, I have acquired a deeper appreciation of the culture of the Ute. I have learned that there is more to the trees than just the physical tree. The location of the tree is also important, or as mentioned in the book *Comanche Marker Trees of Texas,* by Steve Housers, Linda Pelon and Jimmy Arterberry, "the reading of the landscape." One must study how the tree connects to the geology, hydrology, and topography. Is it on a ridgeline or trail; are there other CMTs in the area; what is the importance of the area? What are the surroundings telling us regarding why the Ute selected a tree and its particular location? Like pieces of a jigsaw puzzle, many things fit together even if some of the pieces have been lost.

While revisiting areas that we have previously explored with Dr. Jefferson over the last few years, we noted that we have lost many of the trees we originally studied due to fire, drought, snowfall and natural causes such as age. Ancient CMTs one day will all be gone. When talking to Dr. Jefferson about the role that non-Ute people can take in preserving the trees and educating the public regarding their importance, his guidance is that our role should focus today on documenting the trees through photography and mapping. His vision is that our information and documentation will one day help the Ute locate trees for their cultural teaching and lead to the reunification with the trees for both present and future generations of Ute. These trees are living Native American artifacts.

As pointed out by Dr. Jefferson and also in an interview with Ute Alden Naranjo found in the book *Ute Indian Arts and Culture: From Prehistory to the New Millennium* published by the Colorado Springs Fine Arts Center, Native American youth are more interested in what is happening in the present, like sports, movies and fashion. Most youth are often not interested in their culture. Whether it is Ute youth or any culture's youth, modern computers, video games and events hold their interest, and it is important that stories, customs and history be recorded for their future. It is only as children mature that some become interested in their culture. My hope in recording CMTs, their location and proximity to other historic sites is that I can help with Dr. Jefferson's vision and that the location of these natural artifacts will be on record for Ute to find in the future.

The Challenge and Conflict of Categorizing Culturally Modified Trees

There is not yet a consensus, either on or off the Ute Reservations, as to how many categories of Culturally Modified Trees can be contributed to the Ute, if any. There is no doubt that Native Americans modified trees and that the Ute were the predominant tribe in the Rocky Mountains and that they modified trees. It is the attributing to whom and interpreting why and classifying the different types of trees, for understanding and teaching purposes, that has become challenging and controversial. The Colorado State Archaeologist, as of the writing of this book, recognizes only two types of Culturally Modified Trees: those modified for medicinal or nutritional purposes and those that have been carved to tell a story or for navigational purposes. These trees are referred to as Peeled Trees and Arborglyph Trees. The Colorado State Archaeologist does not recognize Trailmarker Trees, bent trees, the most identified and acknowledged Native American CMT throughout North America.

Not being recognized scientifically, or through a certified archaeologist, does not mean that other types of Culturally Modified Trees do not exist. As with most Native American cultures, the Ute had no written language and depended on their oral history being passed down from one generation to the next. Many Elders are concerned their tribal culture and traditions are diminishing with the passing of each generation and today are sharing with their youth the history of their ancestors concerning CMTs and their spiritual meaning. Some Ute Elders agree that teaching future generations about the modified trees before they are all gone is of great importance. Sadly, as with the ancient Ute, one day all the Ute Prayer Trees (UPTs) will be gone from either forest fires, fire mitigation, natural effects such as snowfall or even the life expectancy of the tree. Some trees are destroyed simply due to a lack of awareness or are destroyed as we continue to build roadways, power lines and developments. What specific name the trees are called is important for identification and understanding, but not as important as the history and preservation of the trees. I have found during my studies of CMTs that similar looking trees are called by various names by different tribal members. Many trees can fall into more than one category. Identified in my book *Ute Prayer Trees of the Pikes Peak Region,* and again in this book, we will look at the five generally accepted categories of CMTs and various different names ascribed to them. When we are walking and talking with Ute, many give a name to an individual tree, like a name we call a person, not a category. "We call this tree Grandmother" or "This one is called The Holy Woman."

Another challenge that has made it difficult to understand the Ute CMTs is the inconsistency in teachings between one Ute family or generation and another. This is partly due to the Ute being forced onto three reservations located in two separate states. Some Ute Elders of today remember their Elders talking about the trees, others do not. Throughout the United States CMTs have been recognized by various tribes, but seeking an understanding of the Ute practices of modifying trees has been difficult, especially for someone who is not Native American. During a trip to the four corners area of Colorado for research regarding Ute CMTs, Dr. Jefferson made arrangements for us to visit the Ute Mountain Ute Reservation and eat lunch as part of a three-day weekend devoted to research. During the lunch there was a panel discussion regarding Ute Prayer Trees. The importance of that panel was a beginning point in sharing further information regarding tree modification traditions. That panel was important because a person from each Ute reservation attended. The panel consisted of Dr. Jefferson, a Southern Ute Elder; Bob Chapoose, a Northern Ute Elder; and Terry Knight, the Cultural Preservation Officer of the Ute Mountain Ute Reservation. Dr. Jefferson stated that it is highly unusual to get people together from all three reservations at one time, let alone to discuss a topic such as trees.

During the panel discussion, Terry Knight stood up and said he was once at the United States Air Force Academy near Pikes Peak and was asked if he knew the meaning of a tree in that location that was supposed to be a Ute tree, which some people call a Prayer Tree. He had to say he had never seen or heard of Prayer Trees. His family and his Elders growing up never talked about Culturally Modified Trees. He said that other Ute Elders in other places may talk about them, but his did not. He said "There might be, but I don't know." He did know about scraping of a tree to get the sap, which he said was very sweet both in pine and aspen; he had a Ute name for that practice. Now that he has looked at some CMTs, he said there must be a reason that they were modified; he just does not know. One of the major problems is the different vocabulary used not only by educators but among different bands of the Ute. Although Terry Knight did not know the term Prayer Tree, he is aware that trees have importance to the Ute. In a letter from the Colorado State Archaeologist, Terry was named as part of a group of Ute that did not acknowledge Prayer Trees. The sign shown on the next page indicates that Terry does acknowledge important Ute trees such as the "Target Tree." This tree shows the same peeled bark pattern observed on trees used for obtaining nutrition as other Ute Medicine Trees or Peeled Bark Trees.

The marker placed in cooperation with Terry Knight and the Ute Mountain Ute Tribe shows that the use of trees was important to the Ute, although Terry Knight was not familiar with the term Prayer Trees; he knew the importance of the cambium layer of the ponderosa pine. Dr. Jefferson explained not all Ute used the same terms when teaching about the importance of Culturally Modified Trees of the Ute. Loya Arrum, a Ute Elder from the Northern Ute Reservation, was taught about Prayer Trees and took children from Utah into the mountains for many years to teach them of this Ute tradition.

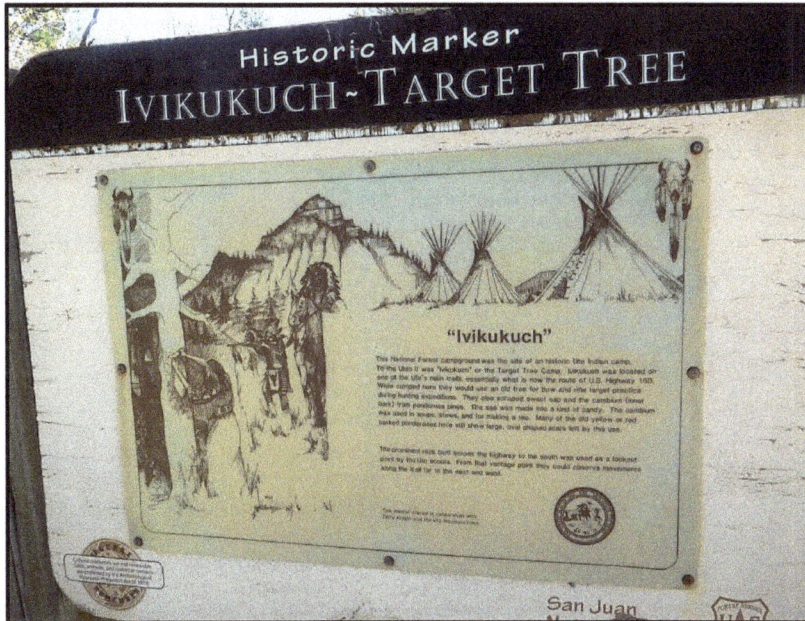

Historic Marker
IVIKUKUCH-TARGET TREE

"Ivikukuch"

San Juan

(Photograph by Dean Waits, used with permission.)

This sign states: "The National Forest campground was the site of an historic Ute Indian camp. To the Ute it was Ivikukuch or the Target Tree Camp. Ivikukuch was located on one of the Ute's main trails, essentially what is now the route of U.S. Highway 160. While camped there they would use an old tree for bow and rifle target practice during hunting expeditions. They also scraped sweet sap and the cambium (inner bark) from ponderosa pines. The sap was made into a kind of candy. The cambium was used for soup, stews or for making teas. Many of the old yellow or red barked ponderosa still show large oval shaped scars left by this use."

It is Dr. Jefferson's hope that meetings like the luncheon will be a beginning to unify the various Ute that are located on the different Reservations to come to a consensus regarding Ute CMTs. With the passing of each generation, this will become harder and harder. His generation is the last generation that can remember their Elders talking about modifying trees. His generation, all in their 80s, is the last generation that was taught the Ute language as a primary language. Language is the underlying foundation of any culture. It is his hope that one day the Ute Nation is able to make a Ute proclamation similar to the Comanche Nation regarding Ute CMTs. This will take some time due to lack of written documentation and differences in oral traditions. The Comanche have a history of modifying trees, and there are documented modified trees in Texas that are recognized by the Comanche Nation. Yet one of their Elders, Robert Atchavit, stated, "I am 80 years old and I'm just now finding out about them." An article, "Making its Mark: Comanche Nation to Recognize Indian Marker Tree" in the *Times Record News*, by Lana Sweeten-Shults states: "Many Native Americans, like Atchavit, never have heard of Indian marker trees, since much of their history was lost when American Indians were moved to reservations and forced to abandon their culture. Recognizing these marker trees is one way to reclaim that history."

Being unaware of a cultural practice previously performed by a Native American tribe is not only a problem for the Ute but other Native American groups as well. The Comanche Nation has a formal proclamation that states as follows:

Comanche Proclamation

Whereas, the Comanche Indian Tribe is a sovereign nation of free and independent people; and

Whereas, the Comanche Indian Tribe, whose ancestors established an international reputation as the "Lords of the Plains," takes pride in our historic past; and

Whereas, the Comanche people lived and settled the country between the waters of the Clear Fork, the West Fork, and the lower White Rock Creek are named the Trinity by the Spanish explorers, and called Pih-heet Pah-e-hoona or three rivers by our Comanche people; and

Whereas, the site of the Indian Marker Tree where this pecan tree grows was a preferred Comanche campsite because of the abundance of water and food sources including buffalo, deer, turkey, pecans, plums and fresh grass for our ponies; and

Whereas, through Comanche oral tradition it was common practice for our ancestors to tie a tree to the ground to serve as a marker and to give direction toward safety and security from our enemies; and

Whereas, the Comanche Indian Tribe believes it is appropriate to acknowledge archeological evidence of our past and takes great pride in knowing that the Indian Marker Tree is a living monument to our historic presence in the Great State of Texas; and

Whereas, the Comanche Indian Tribe joins with the Dallas Indian Community, the Dallas Historic Tree Coalition, the Lower White Rock Creek Neighborhood Association, and the City of Dallas in recognizing the importance of this tree to Native American Cultural Heritage.

Now Therefore, I, Wallace E. Coffey, Chairman of the Comanche Indian Tribe, under the authority vested in me by the Constitution of the Comanche Indian Tribe, hereby proclaim and recognize the historic status of the

INDIAN MARKER TREE

I further call upon all Comanche Tribal Citizens of the State of Texas to observe this occasion with suitable ceremony and prayer.
In the Comanche Country, U.S.A.

GIVEN under my hand
and the Seal of the Comanche Indian Tribe,
this 26th day of April, 1997
Signed, Wallace E. Coffey, Chairman

This proclamation is of great importance as it not only proclaims that one individual tree, the Indian Marker Tree, was modified by the Comanche, but also confirms that the Comanche Indian Tribe's oral tradition states that it was common practice for the Comanche ancestors to tie a tree to the ground to serve as a marker and to give direction toward safety and security from enemies.

The tradition of culturally modifying trees ended approximately when the Ute were forced onto reservations. Once on the reservation in the late 19th and early 20th centuries, the youth were forced to attend American Indian Boarding Schools (non tribal schools). They were no longer to wear their tribal clothes, or speak their tribal language and many were given non Native American names, which is how Dr. James Jefferson received his first and last name. This was an attempt to assimilate and educate Native American children and youth according to Euro-American standards. This was the beginning of the loss of understanding of CMTs.

For the purpose of this book we would like to get past all the problems caused by semantics; we would prefer the CMTs be acknowledged for their cultural importance, not for terms used in understanding how they are categorized. Only a combined effort of all Ute bands to determine the proper terms to use for Ute CMTs will be satisfactory in proper understanding of these CMTs.

Culturally Modified Trees have been located on six of the world's seven continents; the most widely recognized CMTs are the Bonsai Trees traditionally modified by the people of Japan and China. Trees that mark trails modified by Native Americans through bending have been identified in 43 of the 48 contiguous States in North America and Canada and have been attributed to various tribes, including the Comanche, Creek, Cherokee, Cree and Ute.

The Buffalo News of June 14, 2017 reported the thoughts of Jim Bissell of the Tuscarora Reservation on the importance of trail marker trees found in the East. These bent trees are rare and represent ancient messengers to him. "When the Indians did anything it was always for the next seven generations," he said. "When the Tuscarora traveled here from the Carolinas, they planted apple trees along the way, although they would never see the fruits of their labors. It was always for the generations that would come after them." One tree that Jim Bissell saw led him to tell the owners its story. When they found out its importance, they changed their mind about cutting the tree down. It is often through word of mouth that these living Native American artifacts are saved. The white oak that had been modified may have been pointing toward Johnson's Landing, a settlement at Four-Mile Creek and Lake Ontario, where the Tuscarora lived after the Revolutionary War. Because Tuscarora have an oral history, the truth may never be known, but Jim Bissell pointed out "It might not have been a Tuscarora that did this to this tree, but it was a native person. Whether it was one tribe or another tribe, they are all our ancestors." The article did point out that some argue that trail trees could have been formed by nature. Once again, this points out the difficulty in the study of these trees.

The term Culturally Modified Tree is accurate for all trees modified by indigenous people of a region according to their tribal traditions or customs, if semantic accuracy is what is desired.

In working with Ute Elders and learning the spiritual importance of these trees, the importance of prayer and communication with the Creator during modification, it is also appropriate to call these trees Prayer Trees or Spirit Trees as some Ute Elders have called them. Not scientific, but fitting. I call trees modified by the Ute, Prayer Trees, as the importance of modifying a tree with a spirit, for the needs of the People, took much prayer and respect to the tree by the Ute.

CMTs believed to be attributed to the Ute, are listed below in a descending order of the frequency in which they have been found still growing. These trees have been generally accepted as belonging to one of five major types or classifications. The different names given to the categories reflect the various names used in trying to understand classifications, types or purposes of CMTs. These categories in no way are complete, as there are many reasons that a tree is modified by man. Also, as stated previously, CMTs can be in multiple categories; Trailmarker, Story or Burial Trees can all have peeled bark. These categories reflect what I have learned on an ever continuing journey.

1. Trailmarker/Directional Trees
2. Medicine/Peeled Bark/Utility Trees
3. Burial Trees/Memorial Trees
4. Story Trees/Message Tree
5. Prophecy/Intertwined Trees/Ceremonial Trees

Determining CMT versus Natural Causes

Not only is identifying various CMTs by type difficult, determining if a tree has been shaped differently due to natural causes versus modified by man can also be difficult. Prior to placing CMTs into a category, first it must be determined if it really is a CMT and not naturally deformed. When studying a possible CMT candidate, it is helpful to compare the characteristics against a known or confirmed CMT of a similar variety. When trying to identify if a tree is a CMT, look for ligature or tie down marks, peeled bark, color, and other modified trees in the area. Ponderosa pines change color during their lifespan. Starting around 80 years to 100 years of age, the tree takes on an orange color. The older the tree is, the more the bark has changed color. The location of the possible CMT will also help determine if the tree has been modified by man. What other features are nearby? A water source, a significant location such as a rock feature or a trail and other CMTs in the location can help identify a true CMT. Recently I have found it educational to go to an identified ancient Native American landmark and then look for CMTs around the site.

In identifying if a tree may be a CMT, it is worth referring to a short yet informative 24 page treatise by Jack R. Williams entitled, *American Indian Culture Trees, Living History,* in which Williams writes "How Pine Trees Can Become Deformed." Ways that pine trees can be deformed would include: nature interference (weather, wind, snow, cold, lightning, fire, disease, mistletoe, drought, and flood); man interference (breaking, twisting, cutting, logging, and vehicles); animal interference (grazing); and location (rocks in the way of growth).

Dr. Lois Adams, a retired educator, helped me produce this learning tool as a visual aid to help others understand both natural and culturally modified causes in shaping trees. This V-shaped chart is to help "verify" the differences.

Culturally Modified Tree (CMT) Verification Chart (V-Chart)

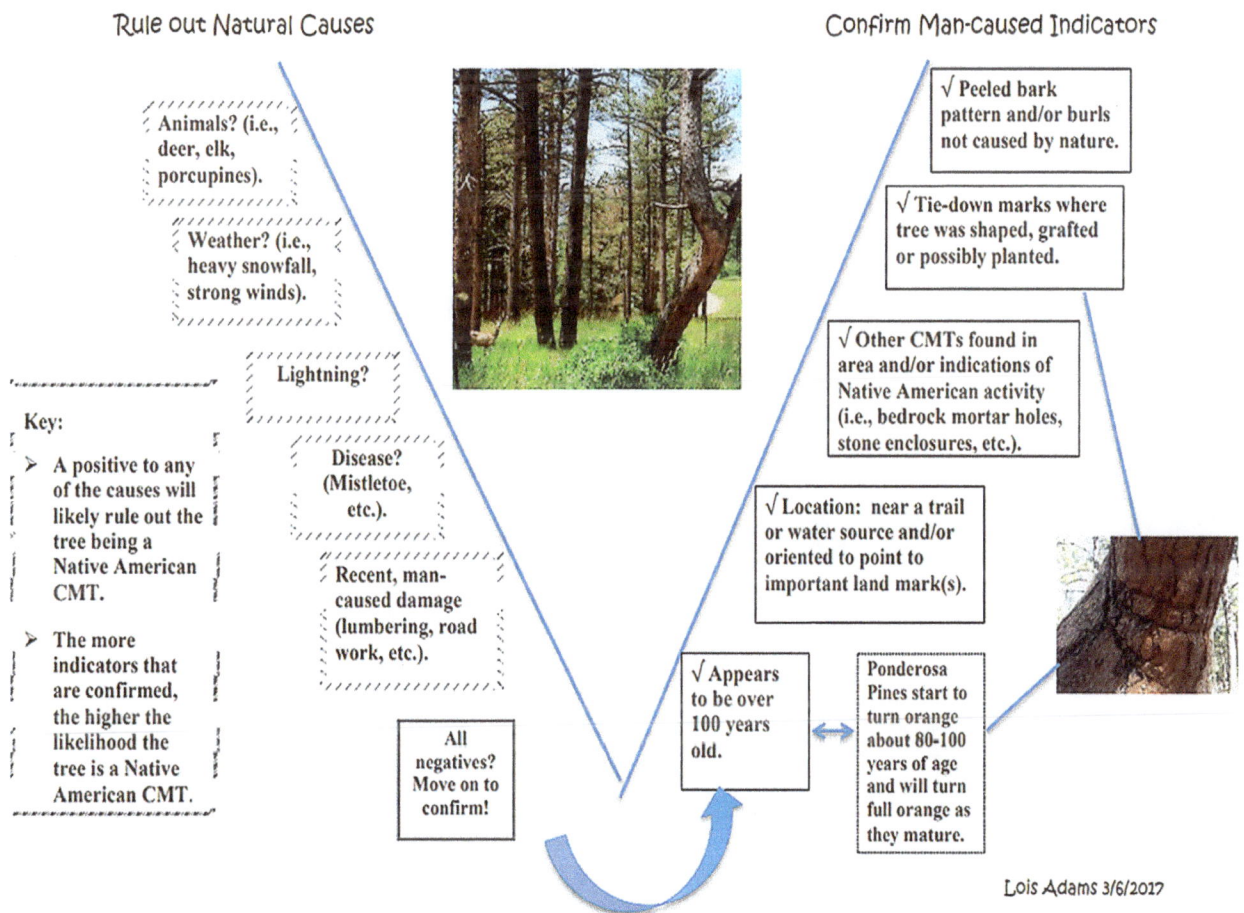

Rule out Natural Causes

Confirm Man-caused Indicators

√ Peeled bark pattern and/or burls not caused by nature.

Animals? (i.e., deer, elk, porcupines).

Weather? (i.e., heavy snowfall, strong winds).

√ Tie-down marks where tree was shaped, grafted or possibly planted.

Lightning?

√ Other CMTs found in area and/or indications of Native American activity (i.e., bedrock mortar holes, stone enclosures, etc.).

Key:

➢ A positive to any of the causes will likely rule out the tree being a Native American CMT.

➢ The more indicators that are confirmed, the higher the likelihood the tree is a Native American CMT.

Disease? (Mistletoe, etc.).

Recent, man-caused damage (lumbering, road work, etc.).

√ Location: near a trail or water source and/or oriented to point to important land mark(s).

All negatives? Move on to confirm!

√ Appears to be over 100 years old.

Ponderosa Pines start to turn orange about 80-100 years of age and will turn full orange as they mature.

Lois Adams 3/6/2017

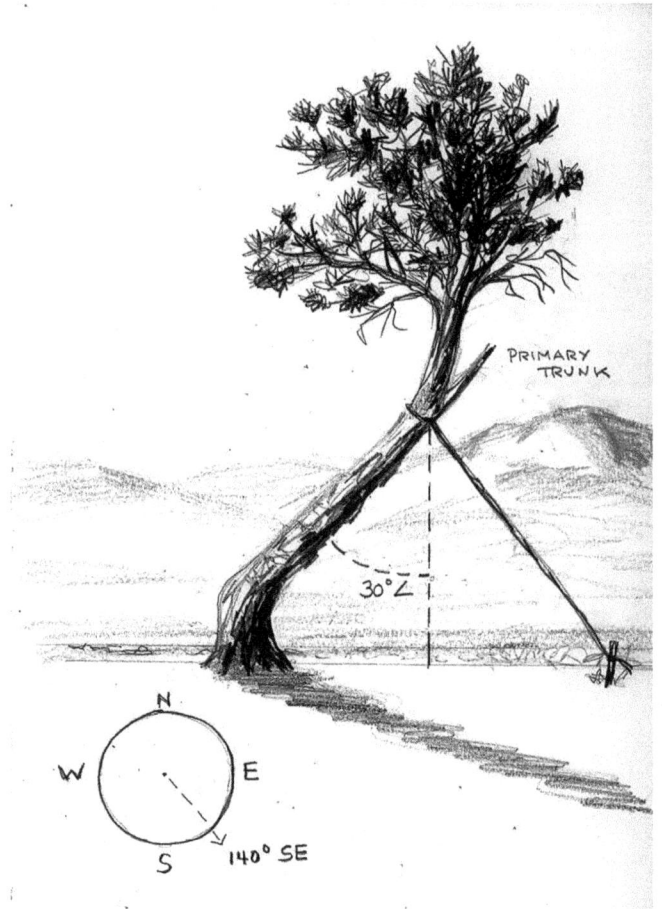

PRIMARY
TRUNK

30°∠

N

W   E

S   140° SE

Y ← THONG

Top left illustrates the peeled bark pattern found on Medicine Trees, top right illustrates a Trailmarker Tree while tied down, and bottom left illustrates a Burial Tree (Illustrations by Deb Bartos, used with permission)

Trailmarker Tree

The first of the five generally accepted categories of Ute CMTs, the Trailmarker Tree, appears to be the most common type and is also known as a Directional Tree. These trees are still observable today in large numbers across much of the Rocky Mountains. The trunk has been tied down to grow at a 30 degree angle, and then allowed to form a new primary trunk to grow vertically to seek the sun. The 30 degree angle is held in place by being tied and staked. The most identifiable characteristic of the Trailmarker Tree is this permanent angular bend of the trunk, always pointing toward some geographical or navigational reference.

Trailmarker Trees can usually be identified by what looks like a dead limb that grew outward near its distinctive upward bend; however, this limb is actually what remains of the primary tree trunk that withered and died after the tree was tied down. A close inspection of the tree's bark at the point along the inside of the modified bend in the tree often reveals a permanent scarring, constriction and/or discoloration of the bark caused by the ligature device that had been tied around the tree when it was much younger and more pliable. The above photograph shows distinctive ligature marks where the tree was modified to bend. One good description of these ligature marks is the term "cross grain scarring" used in the book *Comanche Marker Trees of Texas,* by Steve Houser, Linda Pelon and Jimmy Arterberry. This modification often caused a secondary trunk, known to horticulturalists as a leader, to grow upright off the tree's main trunk, leaving the original primary trunk to atrophy and wither away. Often a small cut can be seen around the primary trunk which was made to impede the growth of the original trunk and allow the secondary trunk to become the new leader seeking sunlight. This practice is called girdling by foresters.

Examination of the trunk located nearest the point of the outside of the bend may help to make an assessment of the direction the tree points. A wider examination of the area often provides further evidence of ancient human intervention such as another CMT, a fire pit, ancient trail, spring, mountain pass, burial mound or sacred site. The direction the Trailmarker Tree is pointing is not random; the orientation is deliberate.

Once the thirty degree bend had been achieved, the ligature devices simply wore away after several annual growth seasons. The ligature devices will not be found intact, but distinctive indentations around the bark can often be observed suggesting the ligature was likely made of natural fiber such as yucca or a leather strap and was cut, removed or worn away with time.

Heliotropic and heliotropism are the scientific terms for a tree or a plant naturally growing straight upright seeking the direction of the sunlight. The terms are derived from the Ancient Greeks who studied those plants that moved in the direction of the sun, a property they referred to as heliotropism, meaning "sun turn." The Ute, along with other Native American tribes, applied this principle in allowing nature to help shape or bend the tree trunk or limb, toward a specific, meaningful direction over time. This alteration was not done without some level of arboricultural skill and practice no doubt requiring some degree of trial and error, and with the Ute practices or traditions such as prayer.

The Ute were very aware that trees grow upward from the treetop towards the sun, not from the ground. For example, if a person who is ten years of age were to carve their initials in a tree at eye-level and returned to that same tree when they were sixty, the initials would still be at the same height as when the initials were first carved into the tree a half century earlier. When attempting to reconstruct how large the tree was when it was staked down, the dead original trunk can provide an important clue as to the maximum diameter and likely where the top or highest point of the tree may have been at the time it was staked to the ground.

The vast majority of Ute Trailmarker Trees were modified while the person stood on the ground; however in a few rare instances, it appears the person may have been mounted on horseback or may have had to climb the tree or build scaffolding. Trailmarker Trees are sometimes found in pairs, perhaps to ensure the survival of at least one or to make sure they are not overlooked by someone approaching from a different direction. When you find one Trailmarker Tree, it pays dividends to search the immediate area for another.

Carl Koehler became interested in Trailmarker Trees when he saw unusually shaped trees while he was hiking in New York. He found a tree listed as an "Indian Trail Tree" on a map and became intrigued. This led to his study of CMTs in New York and work with the Elders of the Seneca and Onondaga Nation to understand these trees. His research also points out the many names given to the trees modified by Native Americans, including: talking trees, thong trees, signal trees and turning trees.

An early history of the area Carl has hiked reports: "The pioneers first followed the Indian trails and from these branched off to routes indicated by marker trees."

Trees in the Eastern United States that have been modified are much larger that those found in the Rocky Mountains due to better growing conditions and types of trees, usually hardwoods. Many Trail Trees in the East have two 90 degree bends, much like Ute Burial Trees, but differ as the primary trunk has often been allowed to grow and the tree is shape looks like the number four. Trees with two 90 degree bend that have been modified by the Ute are known as Burial Trees.

This photograph shows a Trailmarker Tree in the foreground and one in the background, both pointing in the same angle. When marking a trail, the Ute would modify multiple trees in case one was destroyed.

Medicine Tree

The second category of Ute CMT is the Ute Medicine Tree, also called the Peeled Bark Tree or Utility Tree, as the bark has been peeled away from the inner hardwood (known as heartwood) for a purpose; nutritional, medicinal or to use to make a serving tray or cradle board. It is identifiable by the distinctive scarred bark, which was deliberately peeled away from the tree trunk, often by a Ute Medicine Man or Medicine Woman. The pattern by which the bark was removed is very recognizable. The bark always appears to have been scraped or peeled from the top downward to the bottom and removed usually in one large piece or section. The top of the peeled bark section often displays a sharp angular cut caused by a stone or metal tool such as a hatchet striking the tree in an slightly downward direction from right to left, causing a split in the bark, often starting at one o'clock to the ten o'clock position, and usually measuring several inches in width and longer in length, as shown below.

When examining this repeatable striking and peeled bark pattern, we observe that the split is located on the upper part of the bark and often measures 3-5 inches in length, depending upon the diameter of the tree trunk. The left side of this cut is almost always lower than the right side of the cut. This initial strike, which splits the bark down to the heartwood underneath, allowed the Ute Medicine Man to drive two or more stone or wooden wedges downward between the outer bark and the tree's inner heartwood separating the bark from the heartwood. Other CMT class characteristics that can be examined, such as a bend, spur or evidence of ligature marks, should be present in order to determine with some higher degree of certainty if a tree may be a Ute Medicine Tree.

On the Southern Ute Tribe homepage is a link to the History of the Southern Ute. The page describes the various plants and berries the Ute would use for medicinal or nutritional purposes. The site describes how, "The inner bark of the tree is very nutritious and was yet another food source for the people. The Ute harvested the inner bark of the ponderosa pine for making healing compresses, tea and for healing. The scarred ponderosa trees are still visible in Colorado forests. The healing trees are evidence of the Ute early presence in the land and their close relationship to the ecosystem."

"When the Ute people were forcibly placed (on) reservations they could no longer travel on their familiar trails to gather or hunt for food. As more and more elders pass they take traditional knowledge about plants and their uses with them. In the past the Ute vocabulary included many words and their uses for plants. Unfortunately, these ancient words have been lost." Fortunately, many of the Ute Prayer Trees do survive today and can be studied, and some of the Ute Elders still remember hearing about the uses of the trees from their grandparents. One of the primary outcomes of this CMT/UPT research is to help ensure that this piece of Ute culture and history does not disappear from the historical record altogether, especially with the passing of each generation of Ute Tribal Elders.

Medicine Trees are not uncommon and are typically found tightly clustered in groupings that include other varieties of Ute CMTs. Some Trailmarker Trees also contain peeled bark; thus the tree could be classified in both categories. Trailmarker Trees that do not contain peeled bark could be due to the particular band that cultivated the tree not having a Medicine Man present, or the lack of need for the healing or nutritional powers of the inner bark when the tree was modified.

The surface area where the bark has been removed can vary from extending just a few inches to several feet in length and is almost always found along the uppermost surface of the tree trunk or along the upper surfaces of a limb or sometimes both. This removal pattern is distinct in that the lower portion of the bark is tapered downward, while the upper or top area displays a very distinct sharp cut extending in an upwards angle that sometimes gives an inverted "V" at the top and an "U" shape pointing down the tree trunk.

Some trees have been observed with the bark removed twenty or more feet above the ground, indicating the Medicine Man chose that location for a reason and must have been an accomplished climber in good physical condition. A few Ute CMTs appear to have had their lower limbs cut away, leaving a branch extending outward from the tree measuring 5-8 inches in length, giving the appearance these trimmed branches may have been used for handholds or footholds for climbing. One tree in the Black Forest was found with its branches trimmed almost the entire length of the tree and leaning against another tree with a peeled bark pattern where the two trees met, suggesting a Ute may have used the leaning tree as a ladder, although the leaning tree could have fallen against the other tree on its own.

During the winter of 1868-1869, John Wesley Powell, geologist and explorer of the American West, spent several months with the Ute on the White River in the northwest Colorado Territory (today the state of Colorado). On his journey, Powell wrote of witnessing a Ute Medicine Man climb a tree to remove the bark in order to harvest what Powell called a "mucilaginous substance" known technically as the cambium layer found inside the tree between the hard wood inside and the outer bark. Another observation Powell recorded was how the Medicine Man left an area between where he removed bark in order not to cause the tree to die by removing too large of a continuous area of bark. The surface areas observed are generally less than 20% - 30% of the circumference area and never removed all the way around the tree as this would cause the tree to die. Powell describes how this substance was used as a food source, but it was also used for medicinal purposes. Ancient Native American Indians wasted very little.

Burial Tree

The third category of Ute CMTs is the Ute Burial Tree or Memorial Tree, which can be either a ponderosa tree with two distinctive 90 degree bends that point to where the Ute tribal leader is buried or a lone juniper or cedar tree planted to mark the general location of the honored loved one's burial site. The location of the tree is relevant to the Ute person or people who are being honored with this CMT, perhaps indicating a final resting place, a birth place, or a place where an honored warrior may have fallen in battle. When I was first learning about Burial Trees, I thought of one person being honored by one tree. The more I have gotten to spend time with Ute Elders, I have come to the understanding that one tree might represent one death or the location of many family members or tribal members.

Ute CMTs with two distinct 90° bends in the trunk that are usually found close to the ground or a few feet above the ground are known as Burial Trees. They were cultivated to honor a tribal leader who had died or "walked on." These modified trees are important as they commemorate or honor the life and death or passing of a tribal leader from this world to the next. The Ute believed that all life comes from the Mother Earth, symbolic of the tree growing up or emerging from the ground. The first 90° bend in the trunk of the Burial Tree, causing the tree trunk to run parallel to the ground, reflects upon how this person walked across the ground in life. The second 90° bend, which causes the three to go upwards, tells how the tribal member has died and their spirit has ascended towards the Great Spirit.

The Burial Trees observed throughout the Shining Mountains are found with the portion of the tree trunk running parallel to the ground varying in length from one to eight feet before ascending upward. There is some speculation that the length of tree trunk after the first bend and before the second one extending skyward may suggest the lifespan of the person being honored as either a longer or a shorter life. Another unknown is the significance of the direction the tree is pointing, perhaps to where the person was born or died or is buried, but one thing is for certain; the direction the Ute Burial Tree points is purposeful and is not random.

According to the ancient Ute culture if they led a good life they were rewarded after death by joining the Creator, their Father, in the next world. The Ute believed that upon their death, every Ute is met by a spiritual guide who would lead them before the Creator and serve as an advocate for the good they had accomplished in life. The Ute also believed that fortunately, their spiritual guide is benevolent and very lenient on specifically what good or bad deeds they had accomplished in life and that most Ute ultimately are allowed to pass into the next life to spend eternity with the Creator.

The Ute Medicine Man or Woman and other members of the tribe carried juniper and cedar seeds. In marking the general location of the burial site, they carefully planted one or possibly two cedar seeds and nurtured them with prayer whenever they returned to the site of the burial location. Ute Elder, Dr. Jefferson believes that the Ute were the only tribe to plant juniper and cedar trees for this purpose. If cedar or juniper seeds were not available, ponderosa pines and other trees would be used for Burial Trees. They would honor the leader and share the story about what the leader had accomplished in life to the younger members of the tribe. The Garden of the Gods, located at the base of Pikes Peak, is the lower entrance to or eastern exit from the Ute Pass and is still sparsely lined with Ute Trailmarker Trees. The Garden of the Gods was known to have been used by the Ute for crevice burials, their preferred method of burial.

Burial Tree found in Fox Run Regional Park in El Paso County.

Story Tree

A Petroglyph is a pre-historic etching or carving on a rock face and is often referred to as rock art. A Petroglyph can last hundreds or even thousands of years depending upon the hardness of rock, the depth of carving and exposure to the elements. An Arborglyph is a message, symbol or picture carved into a tree. In the United States, Arborglyphs are commonly credited to the Basque sheepherders found in Northern Nevada in the 1800s. The Basque were from the Pyrenees straddling today's France and Spain. They came to the Americas for opportunity. Often their art or messages were found on aspen trees. Due to the shorter lifetime of aspen, under one-hundred years, the messages were not intended to last for a long period of time.

The Ute were also known to carve messages in trees. As the Ute had no written language, pictures were used that told a story. The message could be a short term message or a long term message. The duration required for the message would determine if it would be placed on aspen or a longer living tree such as the ponderosa pine. An Arborglyph is one of the two CMTs recognized by the Colorado State Archaeologist. In working with Ute Elders, I learned that Arborglyphs are just one type of Ute CMTs that fit into a broader category designated as Story Trees, or sometimes referred to as Message Trees.

While the Arborglyph definitely leaves a message, other modifications were also done to trees to relay a story. Some modifications designated a campsite or a nearby water source. Other modifications such as a spiral, a knot, or the way the trunk or branches were modified to grow held a different story. The few confirmed aspen Arborglyphs in existence today are found in museums.

It would be difficult to confirm aspen carvings found on a living tree in a forest today without some other definitive evidence, as the tree would probably not be old enough to have been carved by anyone from the Ute Tribes. To further complicate the authentication processes, other areas of the mountains in Colorado, particularly in southern Colorado, were heavily grazed by sheep. The Mexican sheepherders were known to also mark trees, especially aspen trees, to denote a message such as a geographical boundary.

All Ute CMTs tell a story. The lifespan of a ponderosa pine, in contrast to an aspen, is approximately 600-800 years. A Story Tree made from a ponderosa would last for a longer period of time and might have been used to help the Elders tell part of the Ute's oral history, which was often told in story form. Events such as a successful hunt or perhaps the outcome of a major battle would be retold for countless generations.

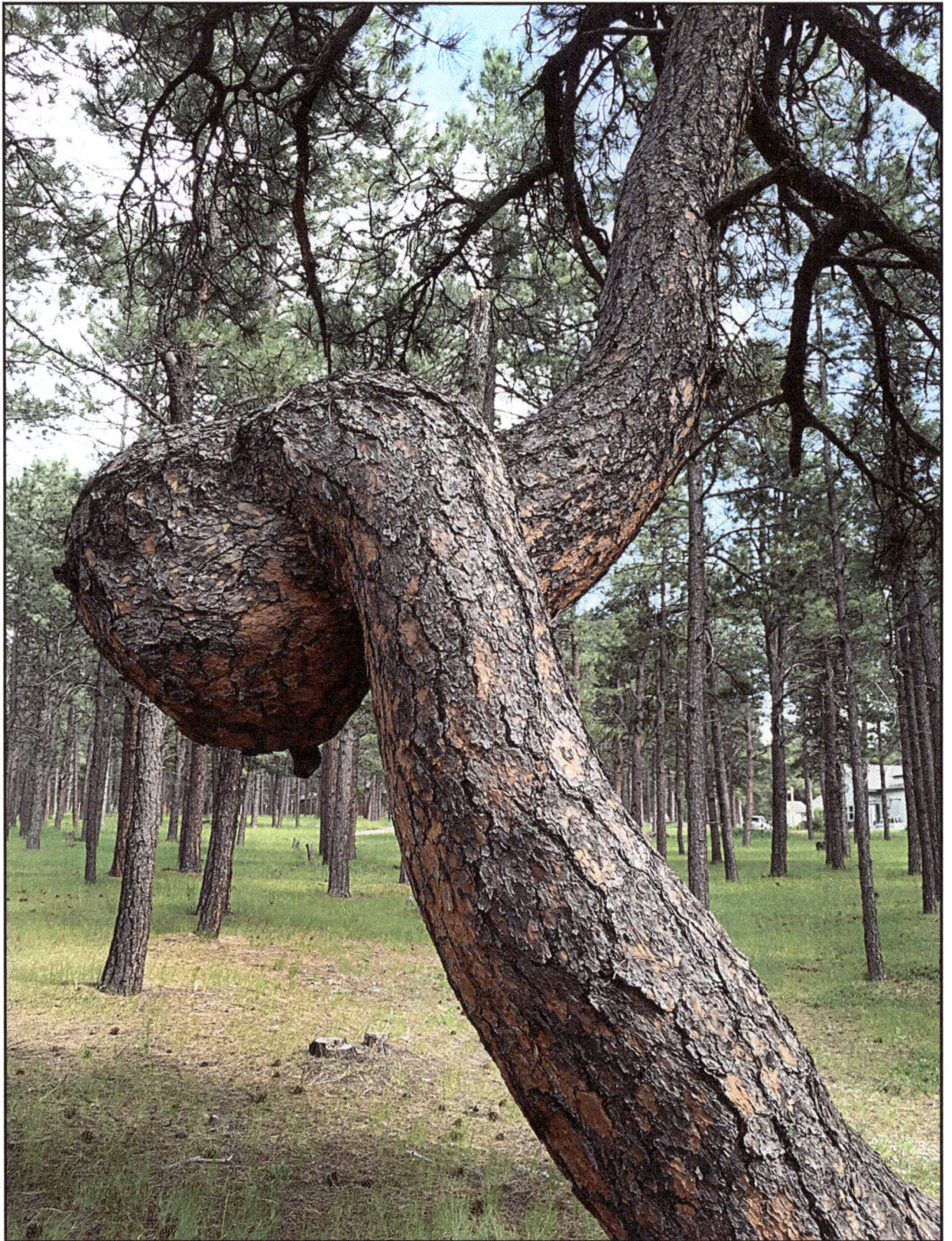

Pictured is a Story Tree in El Paso County. The reason for this twisted knot might never be known.

Prophecy Tree

The Prophecy Tree, sometimes referred to as an Intertwined Tree, is the fifth and final category of Ute CMTs. It is perhaps the most interesting and possibly the rarest, so it is the hardest to find. Where other Ute CMTs, especially the Message or Story Tree, tell of a past event, the Prophecy Tree is believed to be the only CMT possibly intended to foretell of a future event, of someone or something of major significance yet to come. Ute Prophecy Trees are more complex in design and were much harder to cultivate. These Ute CMTs would have required more time, greater vision, and more energy to cultivate, perhaps even across generations.

Prophecy or Intertwined Trees are sometimes found growing together with the trunks or branches fused. This would have required significant cultivation skill with two or more separate trees. While still very young, just saplings, Prophecy Trees would have required periodic grooming or cultivation, over a period of several years, perhaps even several generations of Ute tribal members. Like a Bonsai tree, a Prophecy Tree may have been started by a Ute, then passed on to a younger generation of the family to continue nurturing the tree.

These fascinating trees may have started as two separate trees that were transplanted or somehow positioned to grow together. Other Prophecy Trees may have been one tree separated at its base to appear as if it is two separate trees. The branches of these trees are often shaped or possibly even removed and other limbs may possibly have been grafted from the same tree or extracted from a different tree. The branch may have been connected to the trunk indicating a specific directionality or even interconnected to another branch. On a few occasions trees had the bark split to allow two or more trees to eventually grow together, becoming fused as one single unit or formation.

The National Park Service (NPS) at the Florissant Fossil Beds recognize four types of CMTs; Peeled Bark/Medicine Trees, Prayer/Bent Trees, Burial Trees and Arborglyphs/Message trees. They do not recognize that the bent trees are marking trails or direction, just places of prayer. The NPS recognizes Burial Trees as juniper or cedar trees that have been planted when a medicine person or chief has died. The Ute that I have studied under believe their prayers are contained within all modified trees and while the tree lives, it continues to reach skyward toward the Creator. The Ute believe that when the wind blows, their prayers are released by the pine needles and the prayers are carried across the land for the lifespan of the trees. Trouble categorizing CMTs is a prime example of the difficulty in studying them.

For the purposes of academia it would be advantageous if the Ute would designate categories for each type of tree modified by their ancestors, but it would not be realistic as the Ute believe that each tree has an individual spirit. Although many are alike, they are all uniquely different. Dr. Jefferson has explained to me that although the Ute used similar techniques to modify the trees, they expressed artistic differences between the families that designed the different trees. This can also lead to difficulty in trying to put trees in specific categories. The lack of a commonly accepted glossary from the Ute Nation makes conversation regarding the trees problematic.

The Prophecy Tree is two trees that have been intertwined. Non-Ute people that have visited this tree call it a portal tree as it appears to have an opening from where you are to where you are going. The Ute who have visited this tree strongly feel the presence of the ancestors. Some of the Ute women say there appears to be a temperature change when you pass through the tree portal, and some have the hair standing up on their arms. They feel both a spiritual and physical reaction.

The Stories

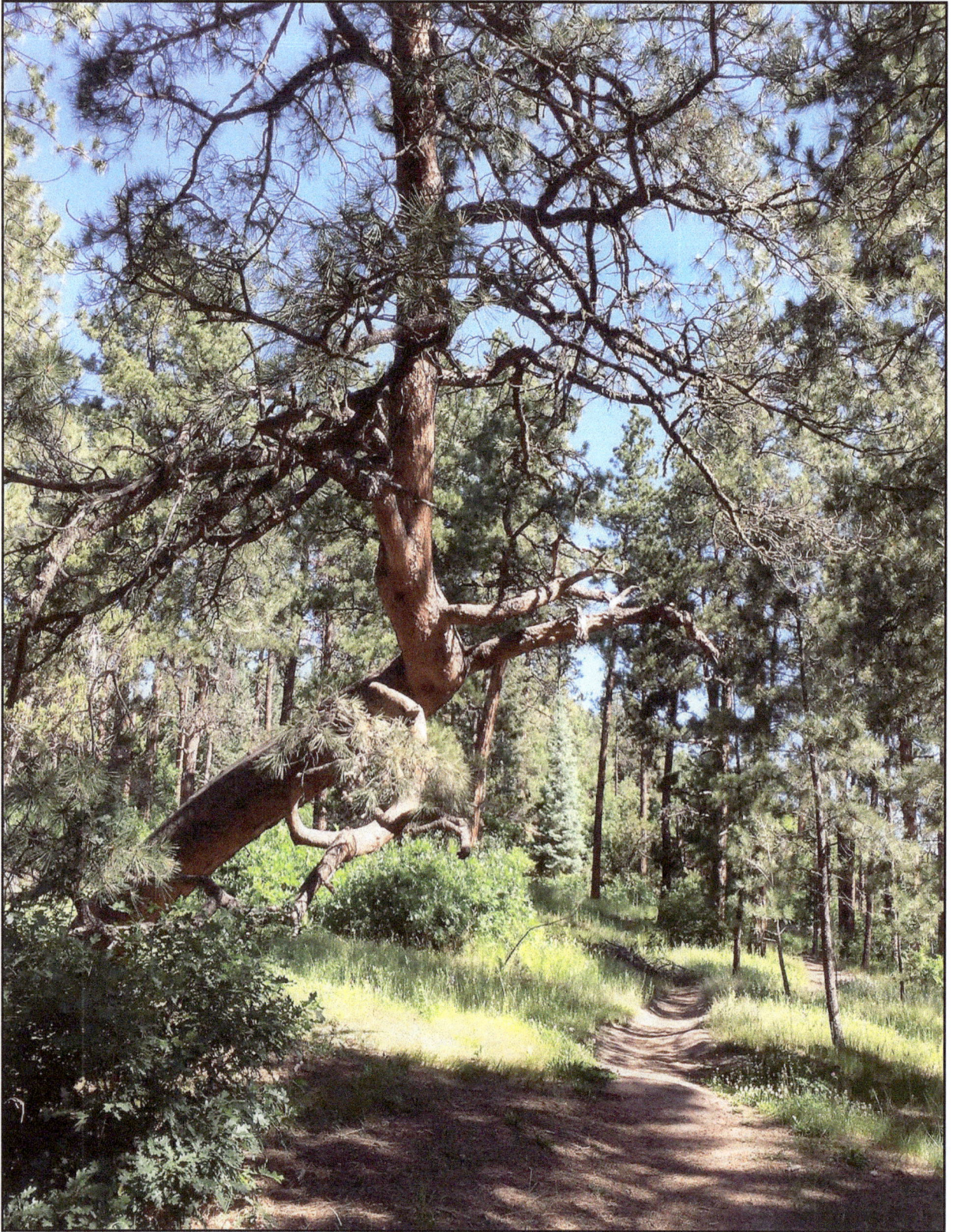

Beulah Trailmarker Tree

Beulah
Pueblo County

My interest in Beulah did not originally stem from the CMTs found in the area. However, it would lead me to one of the most magnificent trees modified by the Ute. Often a side trip with a different purpose may lead me back to the journey of learning about the trees.

Another interest of mine is the American Civil War. Beulah, Colorado was a stronghold for Confederate sympathizers during the war. I made an appointment with Colorado National Guard State Historian, Major Adam Morgan, to learn more about the Colorado Territorial militia. He introduced me to James Campbell, a historian and writer. James was born in Beulah and knew of an unusual tree in the area. Believing it was a CMT, he brought me to the tree to look for indicators that the tree might in fact be a CMT and not modified from heavy snow. The tree had ligature marks, peeled bark and other surrounding indicators. When seeing the massive tree. I knew that it was very special, but always wanting to go to a primary source for confirmation, I invited Ute Elder Dr. Jefferson to view the tree and looked forward to another trip to Beulah.

This is an example why others prompted me to expand studying CMTs from only in the Pikes Peak Region to throughout the territories inhabited by the Ute. This tree was one of many trees that other people have brought to my attention. It was in the Beulah area that my awareness became clear regarding the multitude of people who have the desire to work together to protect and understand these modified trees. Thus, in this book, we begin our journey in Beulah and continue to tell the stories of the numerous trees found in the Shining Mountains of the Ute along with introducing of some of the many people I have met along the way.

Once, Jim Campbell had heard what he believed was a Native American woman singing under the above mentioned tree and asked a friend local to the area, Sandy Christensen, if she knew of anyone that might know the lady. She connected him to a friend of hers who is part Ute on both her mother's and father's side. This woman's family had not told her of the Ute tradition of modifying trees, but she had been drawn to the Trailmarker Tree along North Creek and on many occasions had come to the tree to meditate and sing in her native tongue.

When Dr. Jefferson visited the site, he pointed out that the tree was very significant with its 30 degree modification pointing directly due east. Using GPS we were able to determine that the tree indeed pointed directly east at 90 degrees, showing the human intent when modifying the tree. He also pointed out the tree was surrounded by juniper trees that were spaced evenly, in a wide circle, around the tree.

This would indicate deliberate planting. He felt that this was possibly a sacred site where the Ute gathered over many years, perhaps for a Sun Dance. This tree was pointing to the rising sun in the east. He said the Ute believed that the sun was a gift from the Creator, and we are not always guaranteed a gift of another day, so we should honor each day. Without the gift of the sun, the earth and animals could not be sustained; it is part of the whole. The sun is sacred to Native Americans, including the Ute, and the Sun Dance is one of the two sacred ceremonies practiced by the Ute today.

In 2016 the last heavy spring snow, over twenty inches, collapsed the tree. The community of Beulah grieved for that tree as it was a well known landmark on a local hiking trail. One local restaurant has had a photograph of this tree hanging in their establishment for over 30 years. Knowing how special this old tree was, the town of Beulah had been considering inviting the Ute to have a retreat in the area to bring Ute children to see the tree. On other occasions I have been involved with a group that has raised funds to bring Ute children, along with Elders, to the Pikes Peak region to explore trees modified by their ancestors. The Ute children who have previously come to El Paso County to view Ute CMTs became very interested in this aspect of their ancestor's history. Pikes Peak is known as Tava to the Ute people and holds a spiritual place in their history.

Because the tree had collapsed, Dr. Jefferson decided to hold a ceremony to honor the life of this sacred tree that had stood for over 300 years, pointing to the rising sun. He pointed out that the tree still was part of life by adding nutrition to the soil; it would be home to many living things before it deteriorates back to Mother Earth. On the day of the ceremony, he sang and prayed in Ute at the tree and held a smudging ceremony, honoring the tree not as an object, but as a spirit. When I asked Dr. Jefferson's thoughts on the reasons this beautiful tree fell at this time when people were considering a prayer retreat in Beulah, Dr. Jefferson in his own quiet way, told me that perhaps the tree had fulfilled its purpose by already bringing certain people together.

Another Native American Elder, Leroy Little Bear, a former director of native studies at Harvard University, also gives insight regarding Native American artifacts found in nature. When speaking about the fading of some of the colors on a petroglyph, Little Bear points out that the Navajo create sand paintings for one ceremony that are destroyed after the ceremony. The Navajo explanation is the paintings are not meant to be forever. Little Bear suggests, "It teaches you to be present. Not to take it for granted." In an article by Don Hill in the magazine *Alberta View* in September of 2008, Leroy Little Bear talks about the laboratory of the outside world. Like Dr. Jefferson and many other Elders, they believe that we need to spend more time outdoors to study nature. The trees, colors on a petroglyph, and other things of nature modified by man are passing, and it is important to study and document them while we can.

One side story, during the time when a group had gathered for the tree and smudging ceremony, a Colorado bluebird flew around us and landed on the tree, making noise. Dr. Jefferson mentioned that the bird was just a storyteller, and had a lot to say. He said I was a storyteller, much like that bird. Many of my friends laughed, but I felt proud that Dr. Jefferson felt that way. Over the next year, often when visiting CMTs, interesting experiences with animals have occurred.

Dr. Jefferson felt that the tree brought people together who needed to meet and the next step would be bringing those people to the Southern Ute Reservation for a Prayer Tree retreat. The lady who sang under the Beulah CMT had wanted to reconnect with her Ute heritage and now she has been connected through Dr. Jefferson.

The loss of this tree really made me aware that these are living artifacts of the Ute Indians, and they will not be with us much longer. This growing awareness has motivated me even more to want to document and study these trees through photographs and stories and to make those people who are in positions to protect these trees aware of their importance so that they can be remembered long after they have returned to Mother Earth. Even when the tree has "walked on," as the ancient Ute ancestors, new generations will be able to visit the location of these trees that were chosen by their ancestors to be modified. As often, when one tree is modified, another nearby also has been modified in the same way. Nearby is located another CMT, not quite as large, but pointing in the same direction. It too has a typical peeled bark pattern.

The previous picture is a beautiful Trailmarker Tree found near Beulah in summer. The point where the tree bends is well over six feet high. Right is the same tree the next spring after a late snowstorm. This shows sad proof that the culturally modified trees created by the Ute are ending their natural life and must be photographed before they are all gone. On the following page is a Trailmarker Tree with a traditional peeled bark pattern pointing in the same direction as the one destroyed by snow. The trees are in close proximity to each other. (Photograph by Suzanne Schorsch, used with permission.)

Beulah Trailmarker pointing to rising sun. (Photograph by Suzanne Schorsch, used with permission.)

Sleeping Ute Mountain
Montezuma County

Being able to go to the top of Sleeping Ute Mountain was a privilege I had long been looking forward to, and being escorted there by Dr. Jefferson, a Southern Ute Elder, Robert (Bob) Chapoose, a Northern Ute Elder from Utah, and Dan Clark of the Ute Mountain Ute Reservation was a highlight of my CMT research.

Sleeping Ute Mountain in Montezuma County is located in the Four Corners area, south of Cortez, on the Ute Mountain Ute Reservation. The trip was made while attending a conference that was a joint meeting with the Ute Prayer Tree supporters and the Old Spanish Trail Association. The first part of the conference was at the Ute Mountain Ute Reservation and the second part of the conference was on the Southern Ute Reservation. When the Old Spanish Trail was first blazed in 1776, it followed ancient Ute trails lined with many Ute CMTs. This area is known for not only the trees, but for petroglyphs. Wanting to visit this area for over three years, I found out that it is hard to find any of the sites that are well known by the Ute, without having the proper escort.

Bob Chapoose, who at eighty-three still commands a presence, pointed west and said, "You see those blue mountains over there? That is Utah. I remember when I was a little boy, they would put me on the back of a mule or in a wagon, they would leave the reservation (in Utah), past Moab through the Blue Mountains, heading east, and we would go through the saddle of Sleeping Ute Mountain to arrive in Towaoc." The large, ex-professional football player made the story of when he was a small Ute boy traveling come alive.

While we stood in the saddle, below the elbow of the Sleeping Ute Mountain, there was a view of Mesa Verde to the east; Robert told it was his ancestors who moved the location of the Sun Dance from the top of Mesa Verde to Sleeping Ute Mountain on the Ute Mountain Ute Reservation. The Sun Dance and the Bear Dance are two sacred Ute Ceremonies that still take place. The Sun Dance is in the fall and the Bear Dance is in the spring. The Sun Dance honors the sun that brings light needed for our existence and is a gift from the Creator. The Bear Dance honors the springs as the time of year when the bear awakens from hibernation. The Bear is sacred to the Ute, and one legend tells of two Ute brothers who saw a bear rubbing her back against a pine tree upon waking. The bear saw the boys and the noise she made while rubbing her back became a song that she said she would teach them if one of the brothers stayed with her a year, through the cycle of life. The song led to a dance of the life cycle that honors those who have passed on and blesses those who are newly born. The women of the tribe pick their partner for the dance. In the process of the dance, they can learn about each other and their endurance and compatibility and rhythm.

While leaving Sleeping Ute Mountain, we stopped at the new site of the Sun Dance Ceremony. Only Ute can visit this site, so I waited by the car nearby the sacred site. Bob was very private regarding those things that are sacred and only for the Ute. Many questions I had were not answered but I fully understand why and was thankful for time that he did allow me. During his keynote address at the conference he talked about the perfectly formed tree that they would choose for use in the Sun Dance Ceremony. He also talked about various other important trees, such as the juniper and the cottonwood tree. He referred to sacred cottonwood trees as Prayer Trees. Although not modified, the cottonwood was sacred. He also told us about tobacco made from trees that was used in Ute ceremonies.

When leaving Sleeping Ute Mountain heading toward our next destination, we saw two large peeled bark trees close to the road. Then we saw one up the hill from the road, Bob pulled over and said that I would want to take a picture. The peeled bark pattern was consistent with those examined in the Sand Dunes National Park and various other places across the Ute's Shining Mountains. The trees in the Sand Dunes were well documented as CMTs many years ago.

Later while on the Ute Mountain Ute Reservation we visited the Ute Mountain Tribal Park near the south edge of Mesa Verde. Mesa Verde was originally part of the Ute Reservations before the U.S. Government designated it a National Park. The ancient Ute were familiar with the entire area where Mesa Verde and other cliff dwellings were located as they were part of the Shinning Mountains. While in the Ute Mountain Tribal Park we were shown many petroglyphs. Our Ute guide pointed out many shards of old pottery below the cliff dwellings. He told us that when the ancients left the mesa they threw the pottery off the cliff for the clay to return to mother earth. When the Ute traveled clay pottery would break, so Ute women wove water jugs to be used instead of pottery.

Broken pottery at base of a cliff dwelling.

32

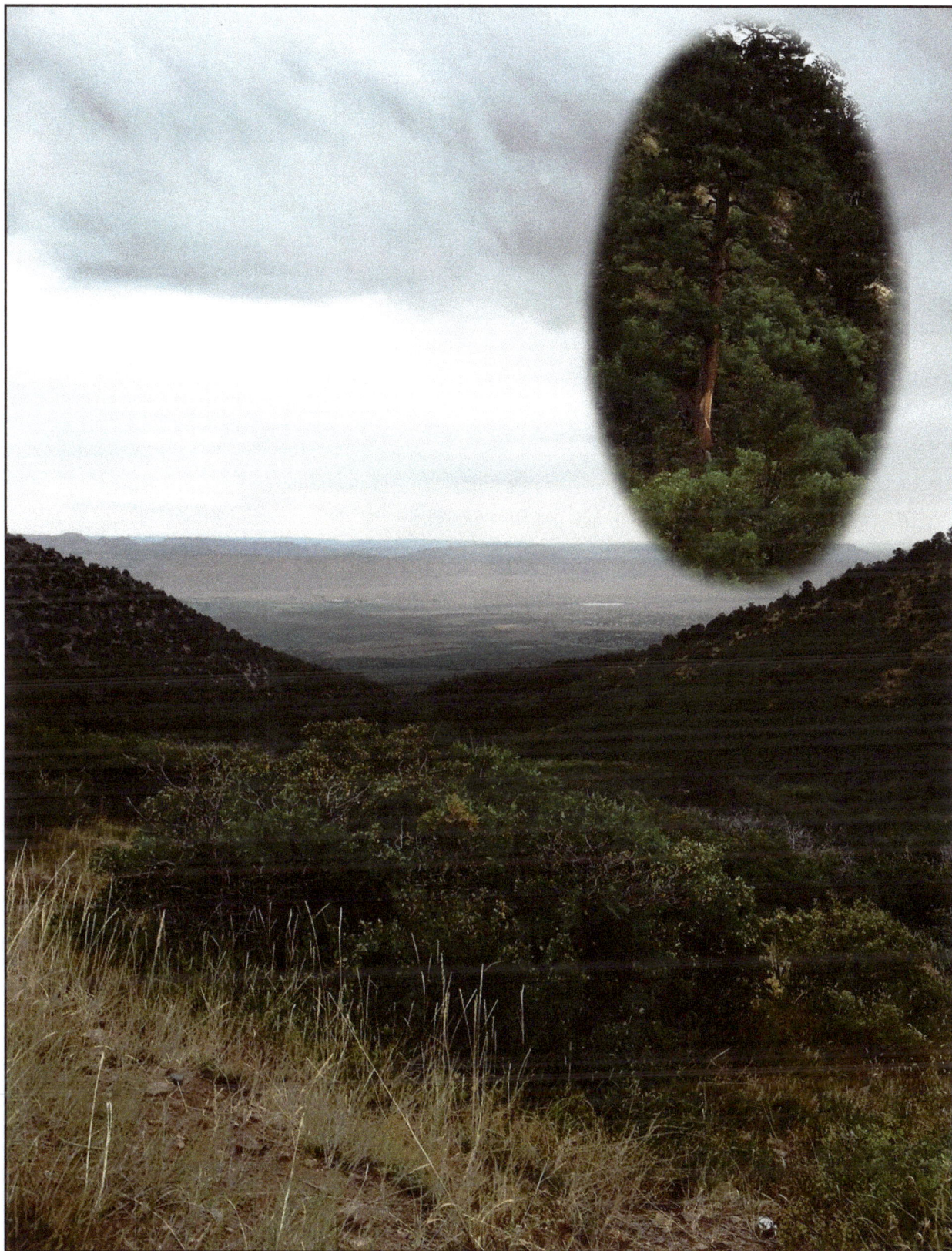

Looking out from Sleeping Ute Mountain with a Medicine Tree with peeled bark, inset.

The Sand Dunes
Costilla County

Dr. Forrest Ketchin, an anthropologist who taught at the University in Boulder, Colorado arranged a visit for Dr. Jefferson, Meggan Braley and me to tour the Great Sand Dunes National Park. During summers off from teaching she worked as a volunteer at the dunes and loved it so much she retired to the Zapata subdivision south of the dunes.

Dr. Ketchin received her Ph.D. in the field of Cultural Anthropology and has spent 35 years studying that area and many years studying CMTs. She explains that Prayer Tree is the English term that Ute Elder Dr. Jefferson and other Ute use to talk to mainstream cultures regarding the trees that hold their ancestors' prayers. It is an appropriate term, as their prayers still live in the trees.

According to Dr. Ketchin, many cultures around the world hold trees in special regard and these traditions are as old as humanity. Traditions related to trees are practiced from the Saami people of Scandinavia who peeled trees for medicine and food, to the totems used to communicate found in British Colombia. The Jicarilla Apache, Comanche and Ute are only three of the many people who modified trees. Dr. Ketchin teaches that western science is further understanding what Native American science has known all along, trees talk. Tradition holds that these trees unite all realms; they are a conduit that links that which is below (through the root system) with the heavenly bodies above (through the branches). The past, present and future are all interwoven. Around the world trees that are chosen to be ceremonial are usually species that live a long time. In excellent growing conditions ponderosa trees can live up to eight hundred years. This is one reason the Ute use ponderosa pines for Prayer Trees. The Ute also prized juniper, cedar, Douglas fir and aspen as they hold strong medicine.

The ancient Ute were very conscious of the eco-system around them and believed that mankind has a role and responsibility to maintain a balance with nature. The Ute utilize controlled burns to better the conditions for things to grow. They knew the importance of valley locations in gathering food. The Ute territory covered the best part of six states. Removal of the Ute from their homelands, Indian school policies, the loss of native language speakers due to early prohibition and the death of Elders have threatened the end of Ute Prayer Tree traditions. Dr. Ketchin along with Dr. Jefferson wants to pass along those traditions to the youth of the Ute.

The Old Spanish Trails were originally all old Indian trails. One of the branches of the trail went through the San Luis Valley where Dr. Ketchin lives. While in this area we visited dozens of large peeled bark trees. Dr. Ketchin talked about trees that had been grafted and contained burls. Grafting occurs when two trees, while young, are forced to grow together by scraping the wood and bonding the trees together. Although many burls in trees are done by nature, as a disease caused by mistletoe, some were done for cultural significance. Although the meaning is not clear, it is believed that they may be marking the summer and winter equinox.

Prayer Trees talk, she explained, if one will listen. You have to look at the total area in which they are found. Other parts of the landscape are telling a story; stone rings, like-kind trees, burls, grafts, and water sources are all telling a story.

On our tour we met her long time friend Fred Bunch, a national park service ranger, who welcomed us and drove us to the northeast part of the dunes to the Indian Grove area. Fred had grown up in the Alamosa area and after working in many national parks, appreciated the promotion back to Colorado. He was very familiar with the Ute that lived in the area. Fred is well educated and very dedicated to his role as a park ranger and protector of the resources in the park. His skill driving a four-wheel drive in the dunes was greatly appreciated; it was an adventure to reach an area of the dunes that can only be reached with an experienced four wheel driver. When Zebulon Pike came down a pass in 1806 entering the location of the dunes, he noted in his journal reference to "Indian Trees" at the same time as he wrote about the sand looking like waves on the ocean. It was amazing to be standing where Pike stood, along with an Ute Elder of today.

There are seventy-two confirmed Peeled Bark Trees in the Indian Grove area. Archaeologist Marilyn Martorano was hired by the National Park Service to confirm the CMTs in the area. Each tree was identified with a brass pin with a number set in concrete near the tree (as shown in the previous photograph) so as not to damage the tree. These CMTs are listed on the National Register of Historic Places.

During a fire that occurred a few years ago, the Fire Incident Commander was given a map of the location of the CMTs. The foresight of the U.S. Forest Service in identifying and locating these trees was instrumental in the protection of these trees from the fire. Knowing how fast a fire can travel and the immense area of the burn, the Commander was able to set up a fire line to protect the trees, and said "We can't save every tree, but we're going to save these." This was where the line was drawn in the sand.

After leaving Indian Grove we went to the National Park Service headquarters and Fred introduced us to his supervisor, Lisa Carrico, the Superintendent of Great Sand Dunes National Park. Lisa's father retired as a Superintendent of a National Park. After a very long and productive meeting, we spent a few days studying the huge ancient peeled bark trees. Dr. Jefferson said these trees tell him when the bark was peeled was a time when his People were in great distress; there would have been much starvation and sickness for his People. Ute used the inner bark as an emergency food source in times of starvation. It is also used for medicinal purposes.

We met with the Zapata Homeowner's Association in the area, which also contains many of these ancient trees. They are aware and committed to the preservation of these trees. Earlier, while widening a road in the subdivision, they inadvertently unearthed human bones near several CMTs. The Costilla County Sheriff's Office and coroner's office were called and confirmed that the bones were believed to be at least two hundred years old, when the Ute lived in the area. Cassandra Naranjo took over from her father Alden Naranjo, who was appointed by the Southern Ute as their Native American Graves Protection and Repatriation Act (NAGPRA) representative, and she was contacted regarding

the bones. The Act facilitates that cultural items such as human remains be returned to Native American lineal descendants and culturally affiliated Indian tribes. Cassandra organized a ceremony for the reburial of the bones near where they were found. It was very encouraging to us to be able to meet with an HOA that understands the importance and their role in protecting CMTs and the culture of the indigenous people who lived on the land centuries ago.

A short distance away from the original burial site is a very unusual knotted CMT. We have seen multiple CMTs that have the look of being knotted, show ligature marks where they have been modified and are near other CMTs, burial sites or cultural rock formations. Unfortunately, the reason for the knot is unknown.

The Medicine Tree also called Peeled Bark Tree or Utility Tree is one of the many found near the sand dunes in Colorado.

This unusually twisted CMT near the Great Sand Dunes National Park points toward Zapata Falls.

Wahatoya - Spanish Peaks
Huerfano County

As you crest La Veta Pass going east on Highway 160, you get an extraordinary view of the Spanish Peaks. A sign as you approach La Veta Pass from Walsenburg points out that Native Americans call them Wahatoya. Dr. Jefferson, whose Ph.D. is in linguistics, pointed out to me that Wahatoya is actually a Comanche name for the Peaks. New friends of mine on the Prayer Tree journey are Manuel Molles and his wife Mary Anne Nelson, both Professors' Emeritus in biology from the University of New Mexico. In 1975 when Dr. Molles was a newly hired Assistant Professor, he was driving down La Veta Pass with a carload of students. As a biologist he recognized the richness of the ridges and canyons on the side of the highway and felt it was a place he would like to live. Thirty years later his wife found an advertisement for a home up on the very ridge he fell in love with many years before. This property is now their home.

Once they had established their home in the valley they wanted to find out more about the area history. They met with educator Dr. Lois Adams from Huerfano County Historical Society. Lois included the history of Ute CMTs as part of the local history, a topic with which they were unfamiliar. They were intrigued because as they learned about the trees they were sure they had CMTs on their property.

I knew Lois Adams from a talk that she invited me to give in La Veta the previous year. Lois let Dr. Molles and Dr. Nelson know of my interest in CMTs and informed them of another talk I was giving. This led to them coming to Colorado Springs to visit and see CMTs near my home, followed by an invitation to visit Manuel and Mary Anne's home to look at their trees.

Old La Veta Pass was originally a trail that was traveled by many indigenous tribes, including the Ute. Manuel and Mary Anne's home is in the valley off the original La Veta Pass and has a wide view of the valley. Two natural springs are located on their property, and today it is home to many bears, causing them to name their home Bear's Home. On one occasion Manuel noticed a bear peeking in the windows of their home. He pointed out the paw prints when I visited. The prints were located over eight feet high on the window.

The natural springs were most definitely a reason for the Ute to use this valley. Along with the springs, the area is abundant with berries, also important to both the Ute and bears. Once when walking down the driveway Manuel came upon a bear that was in the bushes eating berries. Manuel slowly backed away, speaking calmly, telling the bear that the berries belonged to him. He allowed the bear to have what was his due.

Proof of the Ute presence in the area are the very unusual CMTs found on the property. The trees were so impressive that I revisited the site later, bringing Dr. Jefferson with me for his knowledge and opinion. Also of interest to Dr. Jefferson were the bears in the area. Dr. Jefferson is a member of the Bear Clan and is affiliated with the Capote, which is one of the seven bands of the Ute Nation. He knew the valley contained bitter root (Calamus), which was one reason he wanted to visit this area with me when I asked. Bitter root has been used for many centuries throughout the winter for medicinal purposes by the Ute. Calamus grows where it can keep its roots wet. It contains oils that help with digestion and heartburn and is considered a sacred plant among Native Americans.

One of the largest trees in the area, and presumably the oldest, has one branch that looks very much like it has been grafted. Some people refer to the oldest tree in an area as a Mother Tree. Some believe that the Mother Tree's root system has a way to share information with other trees that make up the greater ecosystem in the area. The Ute used the entire landscape as their pharmacy and food source, so they were very aware that an area that contained natural springs would support both plant and animal life that was important for the existence of their People. According to Nathan Strong Elk, the Ute today still track 405 species of plants across their ancient homelands. Nathan is the former executive director for the Southern Ute Cultural Center and Museum in Ignacio, Colorado on the Southern Ute Reservation. He was the first Ute I had contact with when I wanted to learn about CMTs years ago. He very generously met with me and pointed me in the right direction so that I could meet Ute who could be my primary source in understanding CMTs.

In the past, Dr. Jefferson had explained that his ancestors grafted trees, transplanted trees and planted trees. Grafting might have occurred to give a tree a branch that would point in a specific direction when the time it would take to modify a complete tree would take too long, so a grafted branch was used. Another reason could be that a tree that was the proper size was not available, so they used what was available and grafted a branch from another larger tree to obtain the modification desired.

Also notable on the property are the number of ponderosa modified to directionally point to rock formations several miles to the east, across the valley. The branches, which show ligature marks from where they had been modified to point toward the rock formations, contain the peeled bark pattern. Manuel has noticed that the trees directional pointing corresponds to the rising sun and appear to have an equinox or solstice alignment. Dr. Jefferson has said that the Ute used the trees for calendars, compasses and clocks. These trees might be an example of this use. The equinox occurs two times a year, spring and fall, when the Sun crosses the equator and day and night are approximately the same length. The solstice is when the Sun is farthest from the equator, once in summer and once in winter.

On one of my visits Manuel and Mary Anne showed me a grouping of trees that had the tops cut off about four feet above the ground, causing side branches to make the primary tree trunk look Y-shaped. The trees tops had been cut when all the trees were about the same size in diameter. Manuel asked me if I knew why this would have been done. It wasn't till another visit and after researching that I was able to point them to a possible answer.

A newly published and highly recommended book from Texas A&M University Press called *Comanche Marker Trees of Texas* by Steve Houser, Linda Pelon and Jimmy Arterberry discusses CMTs made by the Comanche that were used not only to mark trails, but to point out an important feature needed for survival. The Comanche, like the Ute, modified trees to grow in a desired direction. One form of marking a direction was the use of a tree that had been bent called a marker tree, also called a turning, pointing or leaning tree. As pointed out previously in this book, Trailmarker Trees have many names.

Comanche Nation Tribal Historic Preservation Officer, Jimmy W. Arterbery pointed out that "The Comanche would more likely use a yucca rope to tie a tree, due to the fact that animal hide was a valuable resource used for worthier purposes." He also noted that these trees are called many things but the Comanche refer to trees modified by all Tribes as Indian Marker Trees, and those attributed to the Comanche as Comanche Marker Trees.

The book points out that uses of trees are different for different tribes "such as the Ute Indian Prayer Trees of Colorado, or the Comanche Storytelling Place Tree in Dallas, Texas." Arterberry also points out the consistency of tribes in using trees. "Prior to entering into Texas, the Comanche had migrated out of the Great Basin area, then southerly into Ute territories and became allied to their linguistic relatives. They spent many years among the Ute before entering into the southern plains of Texas. The Comanche brought with them a technique of tree usage that served a host of purposes."

The book reports that cedar trees, when in search of light in a forest among many trees, grow a very tall straight leader trunk that was used in making lodge poles for a tipi. In a Ute tipi, the lodge poles used are the same diameter as the top of the cut trees on Manuel and Mary Anne's property that were cut many years ago. When I was talking with Dr. Jefferson, he said that normally the Ute used 12 to 15 poles for each tipi. One possibility for the topped trees could be for the use for poles. Each tree was topped approximately four to five feet above ground level, and the leader trunk was approximately two inches in diameter. The number of trees that had been topped on Manuel and Mary Anne's property is consistent with the number needed for tipi lodge poles. Another factor is that the trees are on the north slope of their property. A northern slope in Colorado receives less sunlight, causing the trees to grow taller, quicker and narrower searching for sunlight, perfect conditions for the type of poles needed for a tipi. Since I became aware that north facing trees were used and read about the lodge poles used for tipi building, I have found similar trees on the north face of Spruce Mountain.

Dr. Jefferson shared that each pole used in the tipi has a name, number, position and virtue attached to the pole. Looking up tipi construction I found one sources that listed the fifteen attributes poles represent: obedience, respect, humility, happiness, love, faith, kinship, cleanliness, thankfulness, sharing, strength, good child rearing, hope, protection, and the final pole controls the tent from the wind through its flap.

Over the course of many visits, Manuel and Mary Anne have become very interested in the trees on their property and developed the desire to protect not only the environment but the historic artifacts it contains. It was very heartwarming to me to have Dr. Molles, Dr. Nelson and Dr. Jefferson together at one time, and because of the trees, they became friends with a common goal. They have different backgrounds, biology and linguistics, but each has a common knowledge that in nature, one thing affects so many other things. The ancient Ute pointed the way to this valley and knew the importance of the many facets that tied the survival of plants and animals together. In Dr. Molles' book *Ecology, Concepts and Applications*, one chapter covers Mutualism, how plants and animals rely on one another for the mutual benefit of all involved, for example the birds and bees. The Ute in ancient times understood the necessity of nature and man to work together.

The picture at right shows the topped center leader trunk that was possibly used for poles for a tipi. There were approximately 12-15 trees in one area that all had been topped many years ago. (Photograph by Manuel Molles, used with permission.)

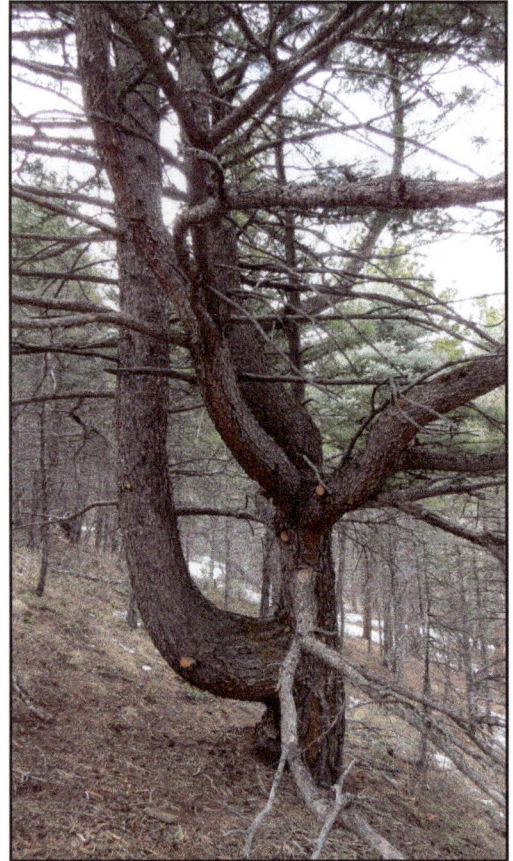

A variety of Prayer Trees; Trailmarker, Medicine Trees and Story Trees are found in the area that surrounds the Spanish Peaks. Another location, Black Hawk Ranch, is believed to have been a destination area for the Ute to gather in the fall to hunt and prepare food for the winter. In the shadow of the Spanish Peaks, the ranch is over 7,000 acres of private land cut into 185 parcels with private roads connecting the properties. The area held a thriving coal mining industry in the late 1800s, of which remnants can be seen. Susanne and Terry Bloomfield invited me to their property in Black Hawk Ranch to view not only CMTs in the area, but other signs left by the ancient indigenous people.

Acorns, found in this area, would be ground to make flour and then with dried berries and dried

meat would become a nutritional meal that could last through the winter. A mortar and pestle are kitchen devices used since ancient times to prepare ingredients or substances by crushing and grinding. Native Americans would find an area of bedrock where either nature would carve out a perfect mortar or a mortar would be chiseled directly into the rocks. There are often a number of these mortars found together in bedrock indicating that people gathered to prepare food. The Bloomfield's home sits on such a location.

Mortar found on the Bloomfield's home (Photograph by Susanne Bloomfield, used with permission).

Bear Basin Ranch
Custer County

One way to understand why a Culturally Modified Tree is found in an area would be studying the other Native American artifacts left behind. Multiple tipi rings are an indication of an extended, seasonal or larger encampment for the Ute. Dr. Jefferson wrote for The Southern Ute Drum website an article dated July 25, 2016 regarding Ute trees: "We traveled from one part of the country to another visiting and trading with each other and other tribes. I call them nomads (traveling for a purpose) and not nomadic (which indicates traveling aimlessly) as indicated in the dictionary. Most of the anthropologists, historians and federal government personnel that worked with Indians use the term "Nomadic" to specify that the Indians of North America traveled aimlessly, which is not true." The Ute traveled to hunt and to follow the seasons and weather. Trailmarker Trees and rock art marked the way. Dr. Jefferson continued, "Some of the trees and rocks are found marking old Indian trails. Others point to water, shelter, stream crossings and more. The techniques for bending a tree into a particular shape have, for most parts, been lost. These 'living artifacts' are a testimony to the skills and knowledge of the Indian people and their being one with nature."

A friend of mine, Dr .Catherine McGuire, introduced me to a Colorado College classmate of hers, Dr. Gary Ziegler. Gary Ziegler and his wife Amy Finger live on part of Bear Basin Ranch. Gary is a field archaeologist with a geology background who has spent a lifetime finding and studying remote sites in Peru's southern Andes. He has taught at Colorado College and Peru's national university and was awarded the title Distinguished Lecturer at NASA's Marshal Space Center in 2013.

Gary knew that there were rock formations in circles on the ranch but was not sure if the rocks were there from pioneer mining times or from Native Americans that lived in the area. When a tipi was built, often a ring of heavy rocks was placed around the bottom of the tipi to hold the hides that covered the tipi in place. Ute tipis were traditionally positioned with the opening facing east to catch the morning's early light. In finding many CMTs and fire pits along with the rings, all within a close proximity of each other, it was our conclusion that the rock rings were not associated with mining times, but from Ute tipis.

Over the last few years I have visited the ranch on multiple occasions with Gary. Due to the size of the ranch, each visit reveals new evidence of the early inhabitants. On one of my visits we located a burial site with one beautiful old Trailmarker Tree marking the spot. Also around the grave site were Story Trees or Message Trees. Dr. Jefferson has also visited the ranch to validate some of our findings. When Dr. Jefferson was on the ranch, we studied a highpoint on the ranch, an outcropping that has two directional trees pointing into the outcropping. It almost looks like the two trees are framing the outcropping. Once at the base of the outcropping a pure white arrowhead was found. Upon being shown the arrowhead, Dr. Jefferson confirmed Dr. Ziegler's thoughts that this was not a hunting arrowhead but one used for ceremonial purposes. Over the years Gary has found many artifacts, including arrowheads and grinding stones called Manos on the ranch.

Archaeologist Dr. Gary Ziegler and Anthropologist Dr. Forrest Ketchin are shown measuring one of many tipi rings on Bear Basin Ranch. Where CMTs are located there should be other signs of ancient people in the area or reasons for the trees to have been modified.

The CMTs near the rocky outcropping, like other sites we have visited, are possibly aligned with the summer solstice, looking through the bowed trees to the west. In the winter, they align with the winter solstice on the eastern horizon. These alignments were used as a calendar by the Ute to mark the time to be spent in various areas before moving on in their annual migration.

It is very interesting when you find a CMT with unusual modifications and then find the same type of complex modification in a different location. An example of two unique trees that are almost identical in shape and modification, has been located in Custer County and nearby Pueblo County. As shown in the next two photographs, both trees have been modified to look somewhat like a tuning fork. The tree in Custer County displays multiple peeled bark patterns on the tree, two of them side by side.

The journey to try to understand more about CMTs has often left me with more questions than answers. What were the purposes of this particular modification? Because the trees are comparatively in the same region, would they have been modified by the same person or family? Was the fork pointing out some location or framing a location or boundary? It is very understandable that when we see a series of bent trees, all marking a trail or a direction, they are likely Trailmarker Trees. With other oddly modified trees, we can only appreciate the complexity of the ancient culture that created them and accept many trees will remain a mystery. The way the trees were modified was not random and when repeated, patterns are evidence of the influence of man, not nature.

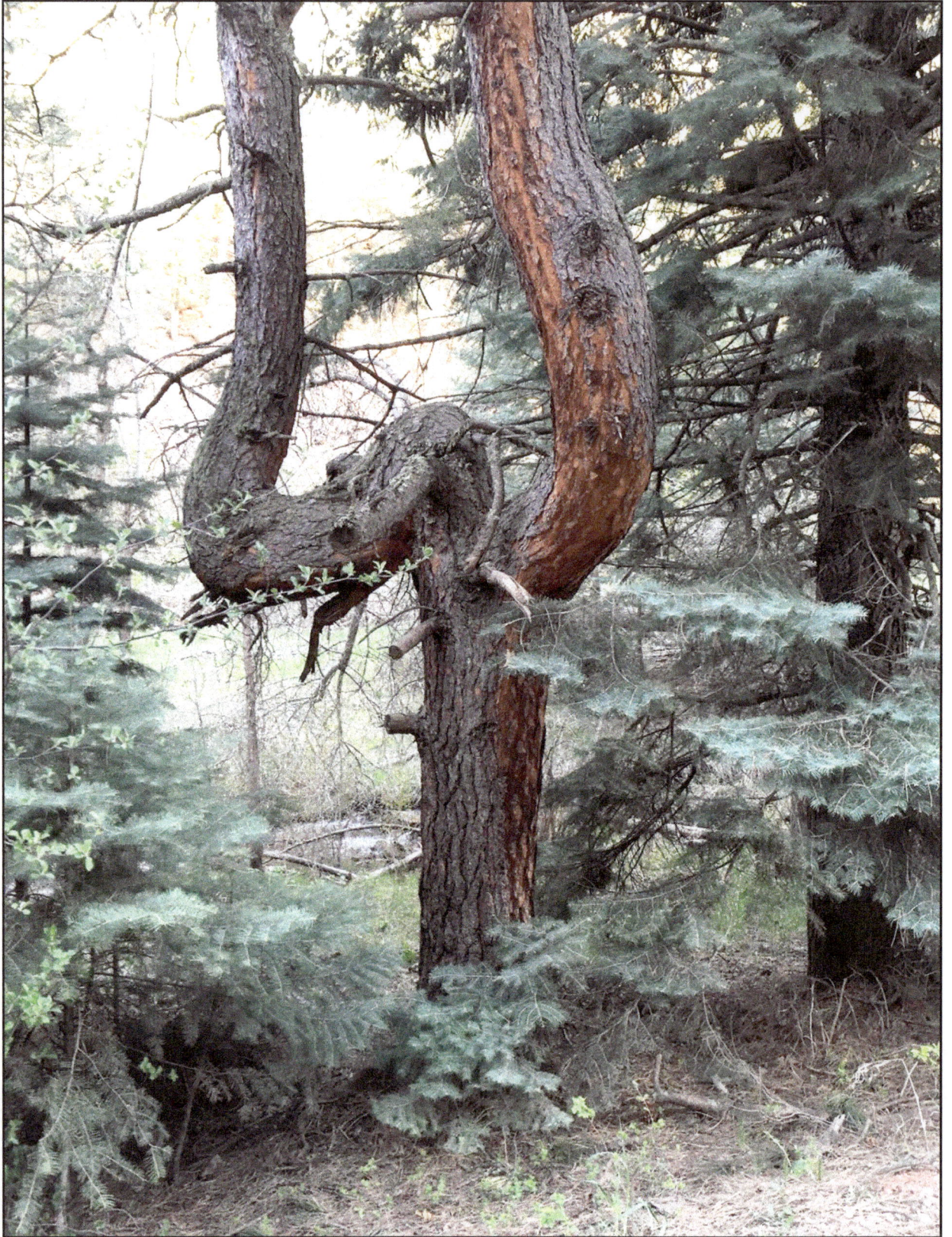

Story Trees with similar modifications in different locations raise interest in their story.

United States Air Force Academy
El Paso County

My interest in the Ute Prayer Trees will always focus on El Paso County; it has been my home since 1956 when I was two years old. It is where my interest in CMTs began. My first book covered the beginning of this journey and focused on the area around Pikes Peak due to its spiritual significance to the Ute People as one of their most sacred places. As this journey has been joined by so many other people from around the state of Colorado, more and more trees have come to our attention found in El Paso County.

One of the people who joined this journey early on was my publisher from the Old Colorado City Historical Society, Suzanne Schorsch. Our early relationship had been consultation on my book on Sheriff Kelly, the first sheriff of El Paso County. In getting to know each other, she shared my interest in culturally modified trees. As a hiker who has often run into these unusual trees she felt the first book the historical society would want me to complete was on the trees. They tell a history that is unique, and as a historian she felt a higher focus needed to be made on these artifacts that are being rapidly lost.

Prior to Ute *Indian Prayer Trees of the Pikes Peak Region* going to final print, Suzanne was visiting a friend camping at the United States Air Force Academy when she found a beautiful example of a culturally modified tree. Not only had the original trunk been modified to point directly at Pike Peak but it has been modified in multiple different ways over many years. It exhibits a peeled bark pattern that is consistent with how the Ute peeled the bark. The tree has also been modified to have a secondary trunk twisted to form a circle, almost giving the appearance of a stool, high up, to sit and have a view of the area. The tree stands just west of Monument Creek, where there is a well known trail the Ute Indians used to travel north and south. Being close to the Family Camp at U.S.A.F.A., it is obvious that the tree has been climbed on for many years by children camping. We have often wondered what should be done to protect the trees from too much abuse and to preserve the trees. Dr. Jefferson believes, like most Native Americans, that all things have a spirit. He thinks that the spirit of the tree enjoys the interaction with children. He believes with education, maybe with an interpretive sign placed near the tree, people would be gentler to the tree. There is a fine line between wanting to overprotect the trees and being respectful to the tree.

After seeing dozens of CMTs over the two years my publisher and I worked on the first book, it was apparent this tree was indeed very special because it was so large, intricate, and unusual, and her excitement in discovering the tree made me want to explore the grounds of the Academy further.

That opportunity came quickly. One day a retired Colonel, Fred Leich, who has an interest in local history and CMTs, came to the Old Colorado City History Center. Suzanne connected us and arrangements were made by Fred for us to meet with Diane Strohm, who was at the time the head forester for the Academy. Diane had previously worked for the U.S. Forest Service. When Suzanne, Fred, Diane and I met, we confirmed that there were multiple culturally modified trees in the area, and we were encouraged that the Academy took steps in preserving these Native American artifacts. The Academy has long mitigated their forest for fire purposes and is very proactive in protecting the environment on the Academy. They are also very active in preserving historical areas such as the early pioneer cabin that belonged to the Burgess family.

Several CMTs at U.S.A.F.A. had already been noted by the forestry staff and have been protected from mitigation. More steps can be taken though; as an example, following the practices done at the Great Sand Dunes National Park, for mapping and marking the location of CMTs could be followed. It would also be advantageous for further studies to map tree locations, mark locations with a brass pin, and photograph and keep records on file of tree locations for future fire mitigation, construction and education purposes.

The Academy, built in the late 1950s under the Eisenhower administration, is a National Historic Site, but pre-history of the area is also significant, not just the trees but any evidence that exists of early inhabitants of the area. This site that has been under the influence of the Spanish, the French and the United States was originally inhabited by ancient people who the Ute believe are their ancestors. It would be advantageous if the Ute would be able to visit the trees that were formed by the hands of their ancestors.

Continued association with staff at the Academy has allowed us the opportunity to be part of working with cadets with Native American backgrounds regarding awareness of the CMTs, not only done by Ute, but other tribes. In the summer of 2017 I was able to take part in an art exhibit entitled "Spirit Trees" that was placed in the Permanent Professor's Gallery at the Academy. This exhibit contained photography, paintings and sculpture depicting CMTs around El Paso County. This exhibit was suggested by Janet Sellers, who runs the Monument Academy of Fine Art, to an art professor at the Academy, Pam Aloisa, and Department Head, Dr. Tom McGuire. It showed the desire to reach out to cadets that have Native American ancestry and study art from around the country done by various Native American tribes. Cadets also displayed art from their own tribes at the exhibit. During the grand opening of the Exhibit two cadets from Native America Club on campus spoke. Matthew Hale gave a Navajo prayer and Juanita Garcia, an Acoma of the Pueblo Native Americans of New Mexico, participated in the exhibit by displaying one of her beautifully decorated Native American childhood dresses. With regards to trees, she repeated this observation, "a life without culture is like a tree without roots."

Diane Strohm has since retired from the Academy but our relationship continues. She is a Board Member of the Friends of the Monument Preserve, which is a nonprofit that helps build trails and maintains trails in the Monument Preserve, still in El Paso County.

Monument Preserve
El Paso County

The Monument Preserve is part of the Pike National Forest located at the foot of Mount Herman just southwest of the town of Monument. The golden spire of Monument Rock, the destination of many hikers, was also an important landmark for the Ute. Along the ridges that overlook Monument Rock are many Story Trees.

At the southwest corner of Mt. Herman Road and Nursery Road is a parking lot and trail head. Following the right-hand branch of the trail along the ridgeline, several CMTs can be located. One former El Paso County resident, Tom King, pointed out that the ridge contains rocks called chert. Chert was used when flint was not available to fashion projectile points and tools. When chert stone is struck against an iron-bearing surface sparks result, making chert an excellent tool for fire starting. This valley is protected on both sides by ridges. It provided water, food and shelter to the Ute. A natural spring is found not far from the largest CMT in the area. These were all important reasons for the Ute valuing this area.

Tom King has spent hundreds of hours studying CMTs in the Preserve. Recently when he moved to the western slope, he wanted his work to continue so he gave the Board of Directors for the Preserve his notes on the trees. His notes also contain photographs, G.P.S. locations and the orientation of the trees. As an engineer, Tom has always been interested in the reasons for a design and has used this in his understanding of CMTs, looking not only to what is on the ground (such as a water source) but what is in the heavens that might cause a tree to be modified. Tom has noticed that the Ute were very aware of the alignment of the solstice in their modification of trees.

One of the many lessons we have learned from Dr. Jefferson is that everything is interconnected, that it all has a purpose. We were sad to learn that Diane Strohm had retired from the Air Force

Academy but our relationship continues and she now serves on the Board of Directors of the Preserve. Only the future knows the purpose of our continued connection.

One of the trees modified in the Preserve has had one branch formed to completely spiral around the main trunk of the tree, almost like it is hugging the main trunk. It is larger in size than the other trees growing along the ridge. It requires multiple pictures to see the multiple places the tree was modified. The previous picture shows the beginning of the spiral modification. The tree points right at Pikes Peak where the "hug" stops. This tree has many spirals. In many Native American cultures the spiral represents the circle of life, or water. It is right near a natural spring. The tree has the peeled bark pattern, one of the largest we have seen east of the continental divide.

Another tree along the ridge looks like a football goalpost with Monument Rock framed in the center when standing on the ridge. Forestry Consultant of over 49 years, Bruce Benninghoff, points out in his article "Morphology of Trees, Natural Forces versus Human Hands" that most conifers in Colorado naturally grow one main trunk with smaller branches attached so that they hold up in nature, especially from strong storms with heavy wet snow. Many things can damage the dominant leader trunk: porcupines, insects, western spruce budworm and Douglas fir tussock moth. When porcupines feed, killing the main leader trunk, the tree may continue to grow for years, but other branches will become dominant reaching for sunlight forming a narrow V shape. One way to tell if a tree has been modified by human hands is looking for signs branches have been modified. Tied down branches deter secondary branches from the upward sunward growth and when forced into a horizontal growth will become new leaders when released They turn upward forming a T or wide U shape, some say looking like a goal post, not the standard V shape. Although many trees will have two main trunks reaching for sunlight, they do not make the wider goal post shape naturally that is made when trees are modified. This is shown in the tree that has been modified in the Monument Preserve.

Bruce has wanted to learn more about CMTs, a subject not readily taught by the Forest Service, and has not only gone on many hikes to look at trees, but also visited the Southern Ute Reservation with me. As a certified forester Bruce has educated me on many aspects of trees of which I was unaware. One is that of girdling a tree. Girdling is when something surrounds or encircles something else. In the case of a tree, a cut surrounds the tree trunk, causing that which is above the cut to die. Then a secondary leader, seeking sunlight will occur. Bruce is very cautious in stating if a tree is culturally modified. He believes that the tree that looks like a goal post at the Monument Preserve is truly a CMT.

Monument Preserve spiral Story Tree. (Photograph by Suzanne Schorsch, used with permission.)

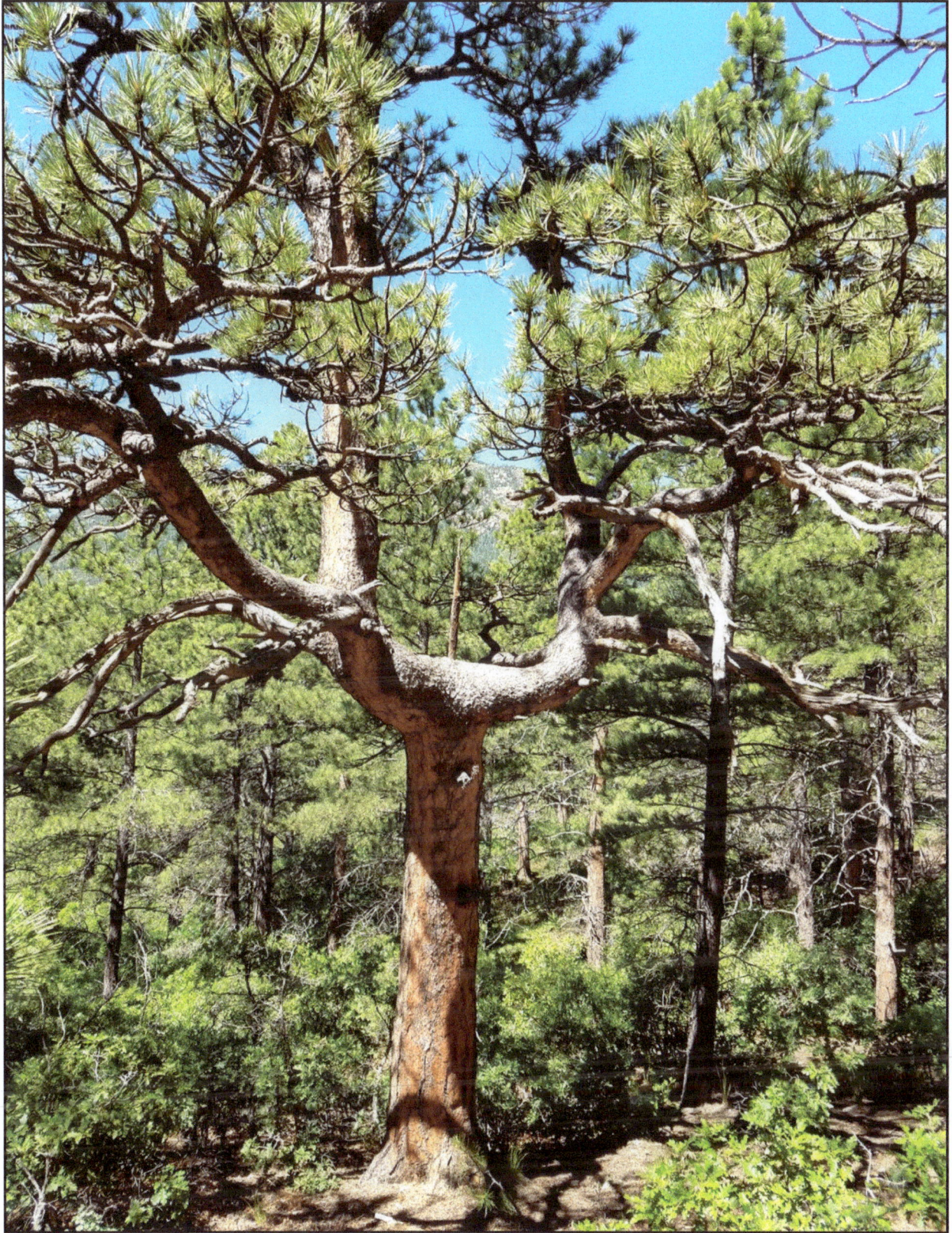

Monument Preserve old growth CMT

Story Trees of the Black Forest
El Paso County

On Baptist Road approximately three miles east of Interstate 25 can be found two CMTs that not only have a story to tell but help us understand the age of CMTs compared to their size. The trees sit on the north side in the easement along Baptist Road, close to where the road changes from four lanes to two lanes. As the road continues to be widened, these two trees will be gone.

As you are standing on the west side of the trees facing east, the north tree has a peeled bark pattern almost the length of the trunk of the tree, exposing the heartwood. Heartwood is the interior older growth of the tree. Unlike new growth, called sapwood, the heartwood cells die. This heartwood is stronger wood and needed for the structural support of the tree. Both of these two trees have been modified with the typical 30 degree angle of inclination like Trailmarker Trees, but they are not pointing the same direction. What are these trees trying to tell us and why do they mark two different directions? Dr. Jefferson told me that sometimes trees were shaped this fashion for field dressing and tanning or for the purposes of stretching hides. They stand approximately 12 to 15 feet apart and the diameter of the primary trunks was approximately three inches at the time of modification. They were modified about the same time frame.

The height of the two trees is nine to ten feet above the ground, and at first sight these trees appear to be too small to have been culturally modified by the Ute, but I could tell by other factors that this was not the case. The coloration does show that they are over one hundred years old, as the bark is the orange tone that begins to occur when ponderosa pines are approximately 75-100 years of age. One problem we have encountered is that sometimes there is doubt regarding the cultural significance of the trees in an area because it is believed that the trees are too young to have been modified prior to the Ute being moved to reservations.

Dean Waits, with the Colorado Mountain Club, Pikes Peak Chapter, lives a few blocks north of this pair of CMTs. Dean leads hikes throughout the Rocky Mountains teaching survival, and as a member of the Colorado Mountain Club he has shared what he has learned about CMTs with other club members. He made me aware of another dead CMT standing just north of the two trees. He was concerned because he knew that the road was being widened for a new housing development and the dead tree was to be taken down. This dead CMT points to Pikes Peak, and has the peeled bark pattern and visible ligature marks. We do not know how long the tree had been dead, but its size was smaller in height and girth than the two trees mentioned above. The overall diameter of the dead tree measured eleven and five-eighths inches.

These two CMTs off Baptist Road might one day be destroyed with the widening of the road.

Because the dead CMT was slotted to be removed, it was a prime candidate for us to date using dendrochronology, the science of determining the age of a tree by counting the annual growth rings. Rings can be wider or narrower caused by drought, weather conditions, soil content and location.

The dead CMT stood on the top of the ridge, in a rocky area that had poor soil conditions lacking the ability to hold water. This caused the growth of this tree to be less than a tree the same age in a different location. One thing we have learned is that trees that live in challenging environments grow slower but sometimes live longer. Those that live in better soil, have more water and better growing conditions will grow faster but often live a shorter amount of time.

Dean approached the developer of the property containing the dead tree to see if he was aware of the significance of the CMTs on the property. Dean was told the trees were too small to be CMTs and that a certified forester had reported to the property owner that the area had been cleared of trees during the early development of Colorado Springs in the late 1800s. What we have learned though is that not all trees were cleared for building purposes at that time as CMTs often were not cut because they were too oddly shaped to use in building. One interesting observation when studying trees in the Black Forest, an area that was heavily cleared in the late 1800s for building purposes, is that the trees that have grown up since that time are roughly the same size. The CMTs not taken for building are often much larger, which shows they are older, as modifications to trees can cause growth not to occur as rapidly as trees left to grow naturally.

Once it was confirmed that the dead CMT would be taken down, we asked Dr. Jefferson's opinion regarding obtaining a portion of this tree for dating. Dr. Jefferson felt that a CMT should not be taken down prior to its natural time. However, using this bad situation to gain a little more wisdom to advance the understanding of CMTs would be some consolation.

We were able to obtain a three foot section of the tree starting near the base of its trunk. From that section cut from the base of the tree, where the tree is the oldest, a cross section was cut, called a "cookie." Dean did a visual count of the tree rings and originally dated the tree to be 308 years old with his second count of 323 years old. The age surprised both of us, as the tree was small in stature. Wanting to get a more accurate professional calculation of the age of the tree we contacted forest consultant Bruce Benninghoff who introduced us to Dr. Lucy Bauer, an ecologist who had worked with Bruce for several years on determining the age of ponderosa pine. Dr. Bauer used her stereoscopic microscope at her lab to date the tree. She counted from the pith ring (year one, the center ring) out in both directions, twice, for a more accurate date. She dated the tree's age at 360 years old when it died. This dates the tree prior to the year 1657. She pointed out the dark ring that shows that the tree survived a significant forest fire and lived another 110 years before it died. The distressed wood after the fire shows a slight bluish tinge in its bark, indicating beetle kill. This tree was definitely old enough to have been modified by the Ute. The photograph below taken by Dean Waits shows the "cookie" of the modified tree that began growing in the 1650s.

Another tree that was going to be cut down due to development in the same area but that had not been modified was used for comparison. It was smaller in diameter, only nine inches, and was 12 feet tall. A "cookie" was extracted and Dr. Bauer confirmed it to be 309 years of age.

One thing that we have observed when examining annual growth rings from a cross section of a CMT, is that the pith ring is offset from center due to the trees modification. When bent, the tree will correct its growth distribution to support the new modified growth weight. This phenomenon is important in dating a tree because foresters are trained to approach a tree at Diameter Breast Height (DBH) to extract a core. Taking a core sample to the center of this tree would not account for the growth rings that continue out from the pith to the physical center of the tree.

After obtaining the cross section for counting the tree rings, Dean took the remaining two and one half foot section and crafted five bowls. He presented one each to Dr. Jefferson, the land developer, Lucy Bauer, Bruce Benninghoff and me as our reminder of the lessons this CMT taught to us, even after it had died. Two of these bowls were put on display at the U.S.A.F. Academy Spirit Tree exhibit.

Examining a tree's age in comparison to its size was a significant event because it gave me a point of reference when talking to people who believe that some trees are not large enough to have been modified by the Ute who lived in the area prior to the 1800s. It showed that using only the size of a tree for dating is not accurate.

One other interesting observation with regard to the two trees off Baptist Road, we noted the tree on the south had small oval indentations going up the tree trunk. I wondered what they were as they didn't appear to be made by nature but looked to be part of the modification of the tree. I did ask Dr. Jefferson if they could be toe holds, or shaped for helping a person climb the tree when tying hides. He said it was a possibility, but he did not know.

We later learned more about these types of toe holds called moqui steps when we visited the Buffalo Creek area in Jefferson County.

This CMT, found in Jefferson County, shows that the pith ring of this modified tree is not in the center of the tree, making it hard to date by coring.

Story Trees are those trees that have been modified to tell a story. Unfortunately, we may never know the tale, as it has been lost through history. Throughout the Black Forest area are many CMTs for which the meaning is unknown but have definitely been modified by man.

One section of my book *Ute Indian Prayer Trees of the Pikes Peak Region* that people enjoyed is the hike included as a means to study CMTs. Included below is the location of a few other CMTs covered in this book; please be respectful of the area and stay on trails.

Fox Run Regional Park, north of Colorado Springs, has CMTs that have been confirmed by Ute Elders. It also is a place to find odd shaped trees that are not CMTs that have been shaped naturally, through lightning strikes, mistletoe, sloping ground, over-crowded growth areas and snowfall. It is advantageous to study what deformities nature causes to understand modifications that were deliberately done by Native Americans.

Enter Fox Run Regional Park from its main entrance on Stella Drive. Turn left past the soccer field and turn left with the playground area on your right; you reach Pavilions Four and Five. Southwest of Pavilion Four are two picnic tables. Just north of the picnic tables is a CMT that has been modified with

a bend that points south. The modification is about twelve feet above the ground. The primary trunk can clearly be seen for two more feet above the modification. Although it looks like a dead branch, it is really the primary trunk that was girdled.

The reason for this modification is unknown but this tree is very much like the next tree. These two Story Trees and others like them have been called window trees as they have been modified to highlight an area, much like a window frame. Although window or frame are not official scientific names, these terms are used only as a way to identify and talk about these trees. On the first tree, shown left, the frame was not completed, but on the second tree, shown in the following photograph, the window modification is complete. The significance of the CMT might be the shadow it casts or what the opening frames in the distance. One CMT that we will discuss later in this book is shaped like candelabra. The term candelabrum is used by another researcher who studies CMTs as a means to describe CMTs that are shaped like candelabra, just as we use the term window. The candelabra-shaped tree points to water, and we have found the same modification in Colorado pointing to water. It is interesting when a modified tree in Colorado is found in other areas, and both have something in common. It is hoped in the future other trees that are modified to form a window will be found, not only in Colorado but throughout the United States so that understanding the reason for the modification will become clearer. Research being conducted on CMTs throughout the United States and Canada is a great benefit.

To find the second tree walk uphill, west, about fifty feet from the first tree. This tree has its window about the same height as the first tree. The modification seems to have been done in the tree's early life. The tree was split, allowing half the trunk to continue to grow in height while the other half of the trunk was tied to grow horizontally for eighteen inches. Then it was allowed to grow up another eighteen inches where it was fused to the main trunk again. When the sun casts a shadow of this modification on the ground it shows a different shadow throughout the day, somewhat like a sun dial. Is the window framing something in the distance or casting a frame on the ground on something of importance? We know that the Ute used the North Star for navigation and for calendars showing the setting sun and rising sun along with the directions. When we study CMTs we have found trees perfectly aligned with the four directions; 90 degrees (east), 180 degrees (south), 270 degrees (west) and 0 degrees (north).

This second window tree was pointed out to me by a friend of mine, Rod Smith. The window of the tree seems to be oriented toward the Spanish Peaks. The Ute had a verbal language that told a story. Rod uses a different medium to tell the story of CMTs in which he is interested. Rod has used his talent with the medium of video and has created three YouTube videos to help people from all over the world understand Prayer Trees. His videos on Fox Run Park, Monument Preserve and Burial Trees of El Paso County have helped educate an entirely new group of people in understanding CMTs. His skills and background are in making corporate videos for training purposes. As part of our journey is to spread awareness of CMTs, it has been a privilege to work with others like Rodney, who use different mediums to make people aware of these artifacts. Another individual who also educates via social media is Barry Trester, who has started a FaceBook page [Native American Culturally Modified Trees/Prayer Trees] which has quite a large following. Both of these avenues are a way to virtually hike CMTs without having to be located in Colorado. They also allow those who cannot get out and explore the ability to see CMTs.

West of the picnic area are other Trailmarker Trees; one Trailmarker Tree points to Pikes Peak. This tree has ligature marks and peeled bark. Another tree makes a complete loop on itself and points true north on one side of the loop and south on the opposite side of the loop according to measurements on the smart phone. The Ute used the North Star to navigate as they were aware that it was the only star that never moved. Depending on where you are located in Colorado, a compass that uses a magnet to find north can be off by eleven to fourteen degrees. Smart phones have the technology to tell us where true north is located, and many modified trees we have found point true north.

Pictured above are trees that bent due to overcrowding and snow fall. (Photograph by Suzanne Schorsch, used with permission.)

Note as you hike that there are many bent trees that are growing in the wrong direction, not toward the sun. Often when the trees grow densely in an area, they will grow a long narrow trunk to try to reach the sunlight. Snow on the top of these spindly trees will cause them to bend, but they will not have the forced modified bend of a Trailmarker or Burial Tree. There are many reasons that a tree can be shaped oddly; those modified by humans show ligature marks and other signs.

This CMT has been twisted and points both true north and true south. This tree is a perfect example of using a smart phone compass to show this tree points north at 0 degrees and south at 180 degrees purposely through human intervention. Note the trees in the background. Typical ponderosa pines grow straight and to the sun. This tree shows ligature marks where it has been modified. (Photographs by Suzanne Schorsch used with permission.)

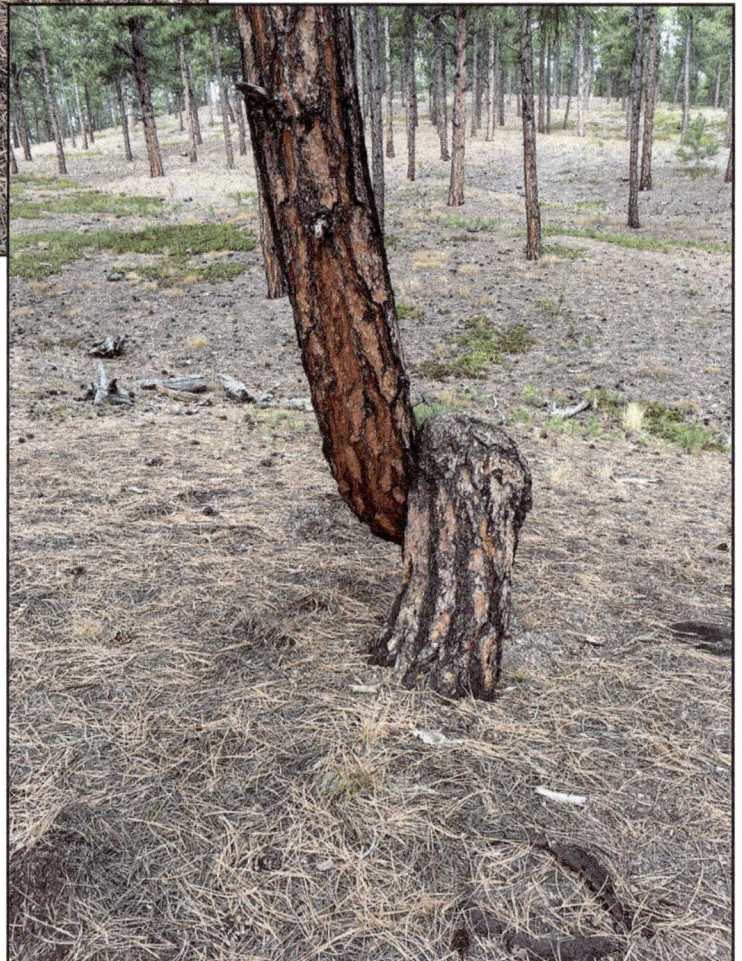

Not all CMTs can easily be found while hiking the trails in Fox Run Park. In order to protect these trees we will discuss some samples, but not their location. For those CMTs near the hiking trails, please remember the saying "take only pictures, leave only footprints." According to Dr. Jefferson, another Story Tree is one he calls an Ascension Tree. It tells the story of life on earth, death, returning to earth, and then the spirit ascending to the Creator, similar to a Burial Tree, but with a definite arch. Pictured are two examples of these Ascension Trees. The arch in the tree pictured in the snow stands over six feet tall.

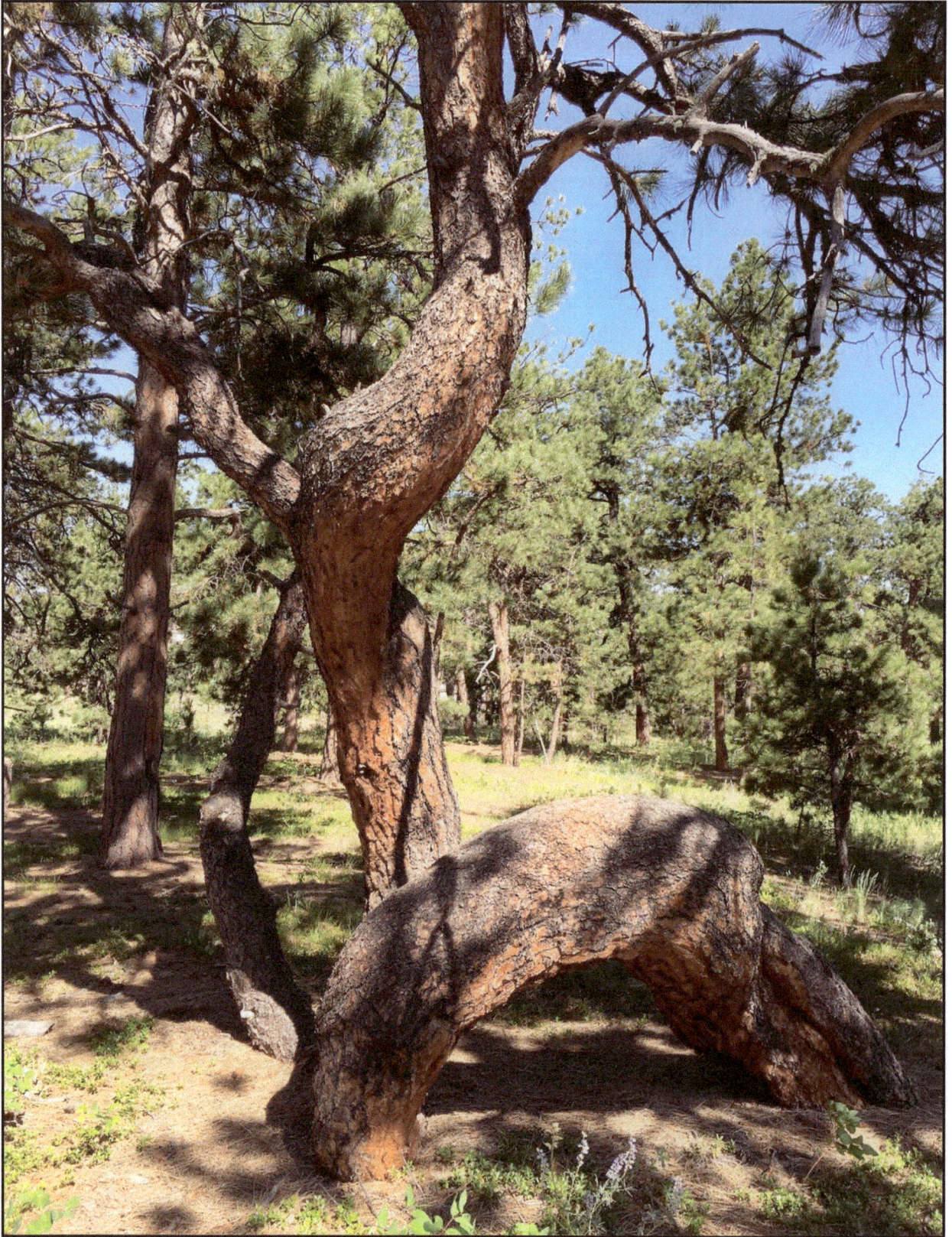

An Ascension Story Tree in Colorado much like the one in Fox Run Regional Park

Along the Cherokee Trail,
Eastern El Paso and Southern Douglas Counties

In Colorado the historic Cherokee Trail followed part of the Santa Fe Trail to Bents Old Fort. Where the Santa Fe Trail veered south, the Cherokee Trail continued west along the north bank of the Arkansas River. When the trail reached today's city of Pueblo, Colorado it headed north following Fountain Creek till today's town of Fountain. The Cherokee Trail then continued north and east to skirt the Black Forest and then went on to follow the east side of the South Platte River. The trail would continue north to connect with the California-Oregon Trail.

This trail was the route taken by William Greeneberry "Greene" Russell on his way to California to seek gold. Russell family members were gold miners from Georgia. When word made it back to Georgia that gold was discovered in California, Russell led two expeditions to California along with a group of men, many who where Cherokee. Greene's wife was a member of the Cherokee Nation. The trail had been used previously and connected multiple old trails used by Native Americans. Its significance was not that it crossed the Continental Divide, over the mountains and on to California. The Cherokee Trail would be remembered due to numerous settlers that followed it on their way to California. Depressions of the wagon ruts are still visible today. Greene would return to Colorado in 1858 following this trail to establish the first significant white settlement where Cherry Creek and the South Platte River come together.

It has been well documented that the Cherokee had a tradition of bending trees to mark trails. In studying the eastern edge of the Cherokee Trail in El Paso County, we find many CMTs. Unlike the Ute, the Cherokee had a written language beginning in 1820 created by Chief Sequoia. He was concerned the Cherokee language and traditions were being lost. The Cherokee did write about their tree modification traditions, one of which was cutting the outer bark at the first modified bend to run the length of the bend on the tree horizontally. They would then make a second cut, across the fibers of the trees, vertically, to help facilitate the bending of the tree. The first bend, was referred to as the hip. Both Ute and Cherokee have been known to make these cuts to help in shaping the tree. Once again we see that multiple Native Americans used similar methods in modifying trees. The written language of the Cherokee helps us to better understand CMTs that were done by the Ute who had no written language, so some Ute practices were forgotten. Although most CMTs along the eastern boundary of the Black Forest are likely attributed to the Ute, there are some that are decidedly different in their modifications and could possibly be Cherokee or other tribes that frequented the area.

When looking at this area along the eastern Black Forest section of the Cherokee Trail, we studied three different sites that had been brought to my attention that contain modified trees. One location is on land belonging to El Paso County, and the other two locations are on privately owned property. Although not all of the CMTs are along the Trail, some are located within the nearby forest. The tree line between the mountains, forest and plains would have been an important location to many Native Tribes. The trees offered protection and the plains provided bison. This was a primary site to hunt long before the Cherokee led the Greene Russell Party.

The largest CMT tree I have seen to date, shown left, sits three quarters of a mile west of the Cherokee Trail. It is not close to the trail, but found in the nearby forest. The shape is consistent with that of a Ute Burial Tree. This tree had two modification points that forced the tree to not only bend, but then held it to grow parallel to the ground for another six or seven feet. The Cherokee wrote about a thong that was used to hold a tree down to grow along the ground. It is believed that the Ute used this technique also. This mammoth tree was modified before the Cherokee were known to be in Colorado. There are two CMTs close to this tree that were not modified at the same time, as they are smaller. One is a classically shaped Ute Trailmarker Tree pointing due east and the second is a twisted knot Story Tree that points north/south, very similar to the one we discussed in Fox Run Park.

Another location right on the Cherokee Trail contains a group of CMTs unlike any Ute modified trees that I have seen. That is not to say that they were not modified by the Ute, but because other trees modified like this have not been located in the Rocky Mountains as of yet, it is my opinion this group of trees may have been modified by another tribe, such as the Cherokee. The age of this group would allow for the Cherokee to have modified the trees, but until other trees with this particular type of modification can be found, their possible origins will not be known. This grouping is found 50 yards west from the Cherokee Trail. They point south to where the Cherokee Trail follows Fountain Creek and then on to connect to the Santa Fe Trail which runs east/west along the Arkansas River. It is as if the four trees are pointing the way home. Questions arise: who modified them and what were the reasons the four trees are pointing this direction or modified this particular way?

Just as Trailmarker Trees and trails connected people and places, looking for CMTs along trails has connected me with people and places that I would never have met or visited. A group of neighbors contacted me regarding the CMTs in this area. One lady had been to a lecture I gave on CMTs and became more aware of trees near her home. She noticed the group of four trees and after talking to the homeowner was told of other trees on the property. I was excited when they contacted me and I was able to visit. These four trees appear to be of different ages, and whether they were modified at the same time or modified at different dates is unknown. The trees definitely look as if they held special meaning or made a significant statement. The largest CMT in the group is the oldest tree. One tree has the hip cut and all show tie down marks. They do not have the distinct two 90 degree bends like Burial Trees, which usually stand alone and not in a group. They do not have the one defined 30 degree bend of a Trailmarker Tree. None of them have the peeled bark found on many Ute Prayer Trees. Although they are shaped somewhat like candelabra trees they are four separate trees, not one. We can only wonder who modified the trees so many years ago.

Many of the other trees on the property are Trailmarker Trees pointing northwest toward Morrison and the mountains beyond. Also found in the area was an arrowhead dating to when indigenous people traveled the trail prior to the white settlers that came along the Cherokee Trail. I contacted a

friend, Bruce Clark, for his insight on one arrowhead found about five hundred yards east of the Cherokee Trail. Bruce, an engineer studying archaeology at the University of Colorado, has taken most of the certification courses required by the State of Colorado to be a Certified Archaeologist. He has studied projectile points and shared his research findings, "I believe it is a Hawken type projectile. I also believe it is made out of petrified wood, very common in this area. I would estimate that it is from the late Paleo period to early archaic period, which would put its age at approximately 7000 – 8500 years old. This type of point was used mainly for bison kills and would put it in line with being used on thrusting spears and Atlatl throwing devices. The Atlatl was being used by Native Americans up until about 500 years ago when it was then replaced by the bow and arrow."

Going further north along the Cherokee Trail, in Elbert County is a ranch that was homesteaded in 1867. The Homestead Act of 1862 allowed Americans, including freed slaves, to put in a claim for up to 160 acres of federal land. The Homestead Act remained in effect for more than 100 years. The daughter of those original homesteaders in Colorado married another local rancher whose family

also had a ranch along the Cherokee Trail in Colorado. Their son inherited the ranch and has lived there since 1926 when he was three. The 92 year old WWII veteran shared many stories of the local area. He remembers playing "horse" on the CMT shown on the previous page that still stands on the ranch. At one time the family placed a saddle on the tree so it could be ridden like a horse.

The rancher recalls seeing bent trees on the several hundred acre ranch, but was unaware of the importance. As a boy he was more interested in exploring with his mother and collecting arrowheads on the property. His collection of arrowheads found at the ranch, shown below, includes some of the many artifacts that reminded him of the indigenous people that lived in the area from many tribes. Also found on the ranch were stone tools, shells, pottery shards and fragments of broken pottery.

The modified trees on the ranch are considered to be Ute because their distinctive shape is found all over Colorado. The age of the CMTs on the ranch predates the Cheyenne and Arapahoe that were in Colorado. The family remembers the Cheyenne being on the ranch during the Cheyenne Wars. Between 1863 and 1865 the Cheyenne and Arapaho Nations fought with white settlers and militia in the Colorado Territory. One young family member was killed during the conflict and is buried nearby. There is no known history of Cheyenne and Arapahoe modifying trees as tribal tradition. The Cherokee definitely passed through Colorado but the trees modified on the ranch appear to be older than the mid nineteenth century. Once again, evidence suggests, the only sustained tribal presence with a tradition for tree modification were the Ute.

Spring Valley Cemetery
Douglas County

While most CMTs are located in the mountains and along the Front Range, the area travelled annually by the Ute prior to the late 1800s, it is always interesting to note CMTs that are found further east. Such is the case in traveling along the fringe of the Black Forest in Douglas County where several noted CMTs exist. This area is where the forest meets the plains and where the Ute hunted bison.

One day when searching along the Cherokee Trail in Southern Douglas County looking for Trailmarker Trees, often found along Native American trails, I entered El Dorado Estate and located a large Burial Tree. This Burial Tree was closely surrounded by four trees, one of which had been cut down, probably to make way for the power line. This CMT had the classic peeled bark pattern and on the first bend, ligature marks clearly show that it had been tied down. The trunk had grown horizontally for over five feet and then a new primary trunk turned upward. The original primary trunk had been girdled, the bark cut all around the tree so that it no longer grew, causing a new primary trunk to grow skyward. The four trees that surrounded the Burial Tree were so evenly spaced around this tree that it looked like part of the modification. Unfortunately you could only see the stump on the ground where the one tree had been cut. The trees that surrounded the Burial Tree reminded me of sentinels guarding the site. Closer inspection showed that at least one of the trees had been fused together with the Burial Tree for structural support. It is so unusual to have five trees grow perfectly in this grouping that it made me wonder if the four surrounding trees had been planted.

The house closest to the tree had one of the largest Trailmarker Trees I have ever seen in its front yard, pointing true North. It was so fabulous that I drove in their driveway. The homeowner, Larry Hartman, came out immediately in protection mode, but when I explained who I was and why I was there an immediate rapport and friendship developed around Prayer Trees. One year later I was invited to the HOA picnic in the area, sponsored by Steve and Maria Cowdin, adding to friendships made on the Prayer Tree journey.

Leaving El Dorado Estates heading north on Highway 83 and turning west on Lorraine then north on Spring Valley Road, there is a cemetery that dates back to the pioneer times when Colorado was still a territory in the 1860s. The locals let me know that pioneers were not the first to bury loved ones in the area; it had first been a sacred place for the Native Americans and it was possibly was a site for Ute burials. The early pioneers knew that if they too buried their families at that location, they would be protected. I was told by one of the residents that there was an Indian tree in this area. I looked for this tree on four more trips to the area, but to no avail. On a later visit with friends, one a Ute descendant, I was surprised when she got out of the car where we parked and walked straight to the tree. Was it luck or the tree's spirit talking to a Ute?

Out of all the counties that we have visited, this is the furthest east of the Rocky Mountains in which we have found a large, peeled bark tree. Now the Spring Valley Cemetery Association members are committed to preserving the tree.

Facing the side of the CMT shows the original trunk of the tree that died when it was girdled. The new trunk shows the ligature marks where it was tied down. The peeled bark is on the tree standing to the right. The same tree, on the next page, is shown from the opposite direction. The trunk has been tied down and its horizontal growth is over five feet in length.

Burial Tree surrounded by four guards.

Spruce Mountain
Douglas County

Each year the National Land Conservation Conference is held in various locations around the United States as an opportunity for professionals in the public, private and non-profit sectors that have the responsibility of maintaining and preserving land for future generations to gather and share best practices and lessons learned throughout the year regarding conservation. In 2017 the conference was held in October at the Colorado Convention Center in Denver, Colorado. This conference was hosted by multiple groups, which included the Douglas Land Conservancy and Douglas County Open Space. These two entities, one a non-profit and one a government entity, work hard together jointly to protect the parks, trails and open space of Douglas County.

Field trips are arranged for each conference to different areas of interest selected by submissions of those attending the previous year's conference. For 2017 one of the field trips was "Hiking Spruce Mountain and its Storied Landscape." The hike went through the extensive Greenland landscape south of Denver through forests and along scenic rock ledges at Spruce Mountain where the participants could hear stories of the land and learn about Culturally Modified Trees, geology of the buttes and how Douglas County has conserved the landscape. I was asked to join this field trip as one of the speakers that were featured at stations along the hike. Stops along the hike featured presenters talking about forest management, conservation visions of the I-25 corridors, the partnership and stewardship of the I-25 corridors between Douglas County and the non-profit Douglas Land Conservatory, the history of the local area and information on CMTs. I was to talk about the Ute and the trees on Spruce Mountain.

The hike up Spruce Mountain starts on the northeast side of the mountain and the mountain blocks the view of the Front Range for the first part of the hike. When the trail turns to the south side of the mountain you get your first view of Pikes Peak in the distance, and as expected after studying places that the Ute placed Trailmarker Trees, there is a beautiful Trailmarker pointing to Pikes Peak. One of the things we have learned is that if there is a feature to point out, such as a sacred site, water location, burial site or land formation, a Ute CMT can usually be found.

This tree has distinctive tie down marks forming it to point to Pikes Peak. The tree has the traditional peeled bark pattern. There is another Trailmarker Tree toward the top of the mountain, also pointing to Pikes Peak.

Another CMT found on Spruce Mountain, shown on the next page, is formed like a large Z. It has the 30 degree bend like a Trailmarker Tree, but points north for twelve to fourteen feet, not toward Pikes Peak. Then the large section that has been forced to point north has been tied down to point south for another five or six feet, and then it has been modified to point north again for another two feet.

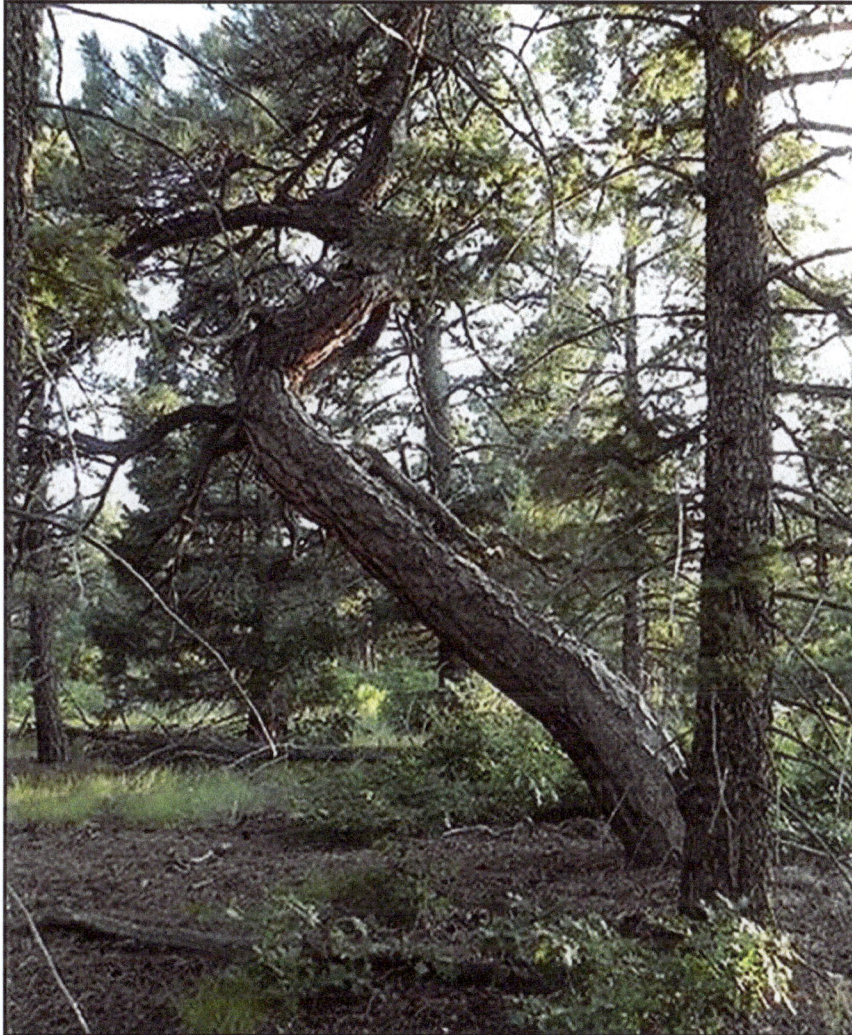

There are other trees along the rim of Spruce Mountain that have been modified to point north. Also on the top of Spruce Mountain is one of the largest peeled bark patterns that I have seen on a ponderosa pine. There is a rocky outcropping about a mile east of Windy Point. The Medicine Tree's peeled pattern starts approximately 18 feet in the air and ends two or three feet above the ground. It shows two cut marks were made to remove the peel, unlike most Medicine Tree's peeled bark that is torn away at the base. The 16 inch width at the bottom of the peel required cutting to remove. This Medicine Tree's peeled bark is unique because of its size and reminded me of a photograph I was shown of two peeled bark trees in Canada that have been protected by the Canadian government as CMTs.

These larger peeled bark trees were used by the local natives to weave clothing, a subject that would come up later during the conference.

The conference was attended by people from all over the country coming together to learn and share information about the conservation of the environment. It is a wonderful dream of many people to have individuals from all over the country get together to learn practices for the protection and education of Culturally Modified Trees around our country such as this event on conservation. What started for me as a journey to understand oddly shaped trees found when hiking has truly become a journey of all the like minded people that I have met along the way. This journey cannot be a single person's journey but must in the future have some sort of organization formed to recognize and protect one of our Nation's historic artifacts. This conference was a good example of people working together for a common goal.

Being October in Colorado, it started to snow and turned extremely cold during the hike. I had only planned to take part in the hike, but was asked to join the opening banquet for the conference and sit at the sponsor tables. Just like CMTs have been modified to take a different direction, sometimes we must be just as flexible as the trees and go a direction that was not planned. Although most people on the hike went to their hotels to change, I didn't have the time and went to the reception still dressed for hiking, looking like a mountain man among the well attired conference attendees. Prior to the dinner I saw another person waiting and joined him. It ends up that Jason Griffith is employed by the Stillaguamish Tribe of Indians from the Oregon area and oversees the salmon fish hatchery of the tribe. He is working on the repopulation of the salmon routes. I asked him if the Stillaguamish had any CMT traditions. He said yes, that the Stillaguamish stripped the trees and made hats and clothing from the cedar bark in ancient times and they are trying to reintroduce these practices. About two weeks later I received a conference call with members of the Stillaguamish tribe who confirmed that like the Ute, their tribe also accepts the tree as a spiritual living entity and they would not modify a tree unless it was done with prayer. They said this is true with other tribes farther north in Canada.

I also met Paul Trianosky, the Chief Conservation Officer of the Sustainable Forestry Initiative, in British Columbia, Canada. This initiative is developing a database for recording, tracking and managing cultural resources of the Heiltsuk First Nation. The project will utilize spatial analysis in Geographic Information System (GIS) which utilizes Global Positioning Systems (GPS) to improve understanding and location and importance of CMTs distributed throughout the Heiltsuk traditional territory. The First Nation people in this area would modify trees to make cedar hats, build canoes and totem poles. Although these CMT practices are different from those of the Ute, this project is a wonderful resource to look at efforts to locate CMTs in Canada and identify and document the trees for the natives in that area.

I guess that like the Trailmarker Trees, I was pointed in the direction of two important contacts that could help me in my quest for knowledge on CMTs. The dinner was not only fantastic but the keynote speaker was Luke Duncan, the Chairman of the Ute Indian Tribe of Uintah and Ouray Reservation of Utah. Chairman Duncan conveyed a sincere appreciation for the distinction and honor of being there to speak to environmentalists who protect natural resources such as the land and water. He said to the Ute, Mother Earth and water are sacred as they sustain life. He felt it was highly important that we all work together to protect the lands of this country that include the homeland of his People.

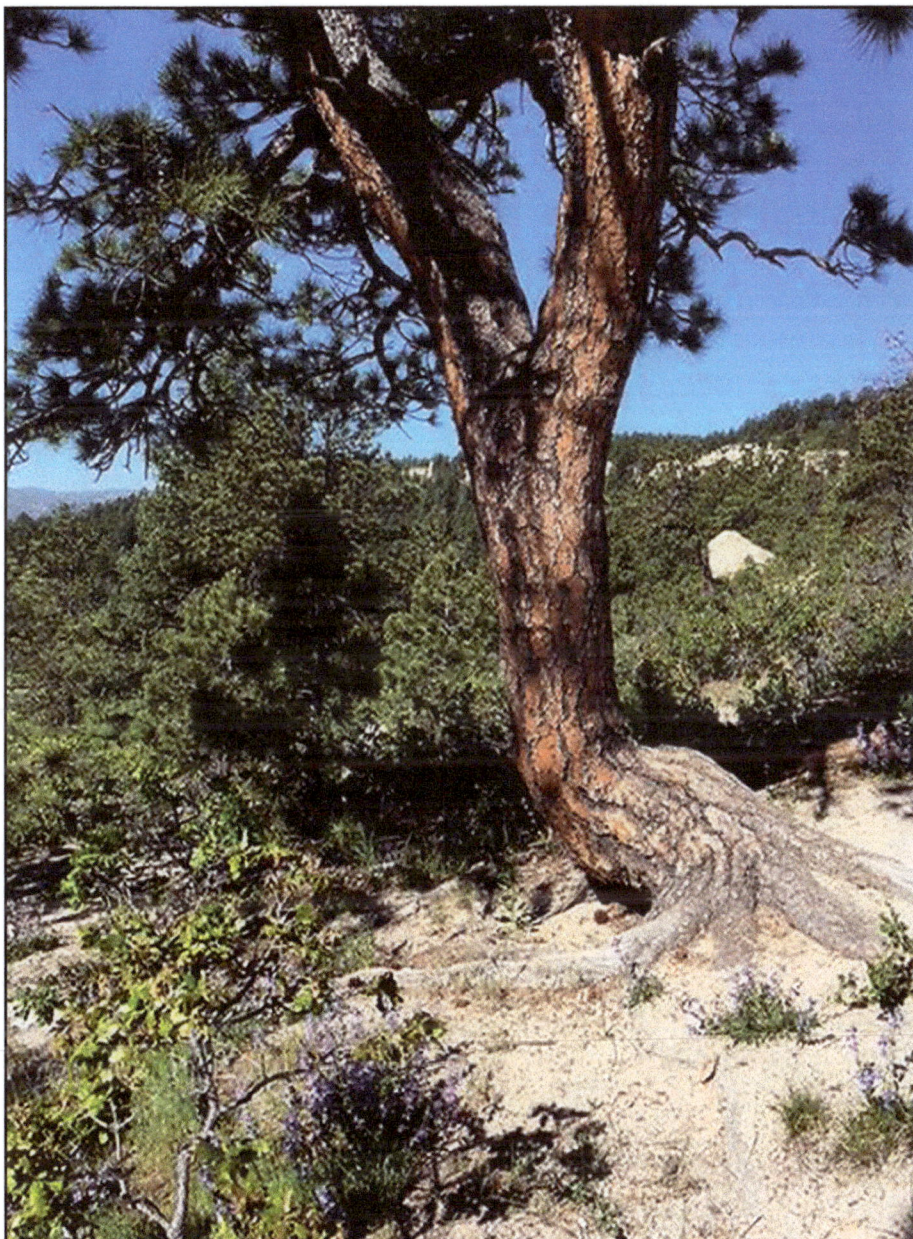

The Trail Tree above is pointing to Pikes Peak from Spruce Mountain.

Pike National Forest
Douglas County

One thing I have learned, when a forester tells me one of the most convincing trees he found that confirms the existence of CMTs is one he wants to show me, I need to take notice. Most foresters are skeptical about identifying CMTs other than the two classifications, Peeled Bark and Arborglyphs, that are recognized by the Colorado Office of Archaeology.

When Bruce Benninghoff told me he wanted me to see a tree that was located on a client's property in Douglas County, I was very intrigued. Bruce was being consulted as a forester regarding fire mitigation and forest management on the private property. Bruce took the photograph of the intertwined tree shown right.

We met with the landowners and were shown two trees that are formed together, pictured in the photograph to the right. The ponderosa pine has been modified to circle, seven times in a spiral fashion. It also spirals around the Douglas fir at certain points. The Douglas fir has a harder wood, Bruce explained, than the ponderosa pine used in many CMTs. Looking upward, the distinct ligature marks showing where the tree was tied to form the spiral pattern on each of the spirals can be seen. These two intertwined trees are over fifty feet in height and the spirals continue the full length to the top. We don't know how many years it took to modify the complete seven circles of the one tree around the other tree, but the tree is well over two hundred years old. Seven is a sacred number to the Ute, as in many tribes, because they recognize seven directions: north, south, east, west, down (Mother Earth), up (Father Sky, the Creator), and center (the here and now). The spiral references life. This tree also

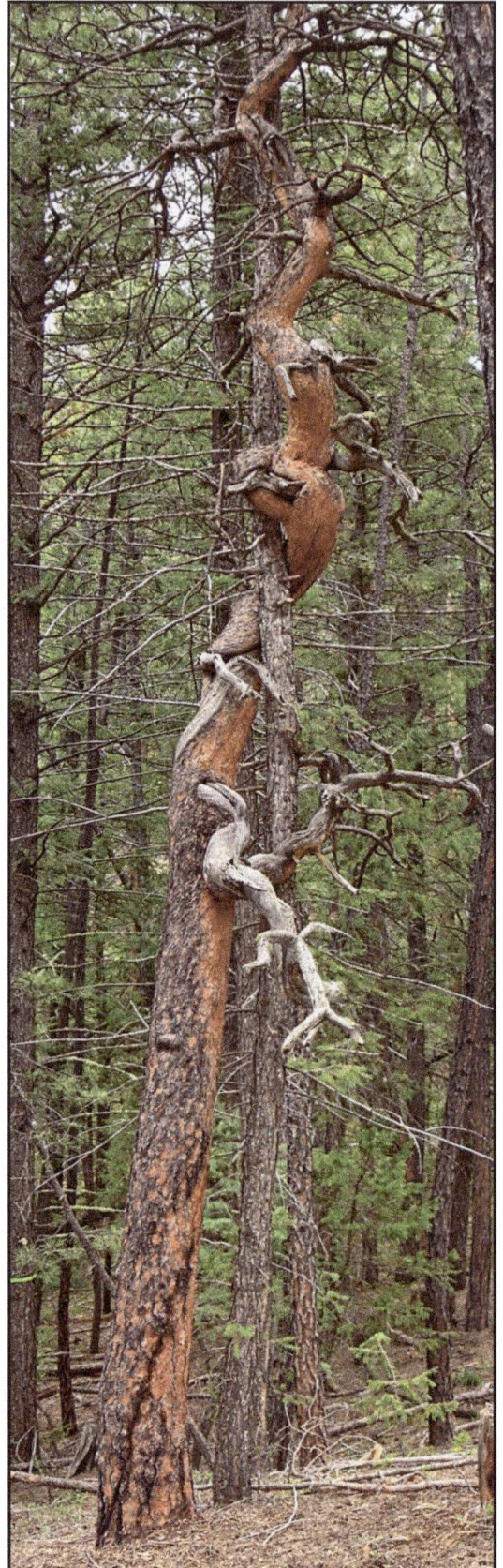

contains the peeled bark pattern. Unfortunately the ponderosa has died but the Douglas fir still lives. The property owner has mitigated other trees around these two trees to protect them.

Like other CMTs, these two trees don't stand alone. Nearby is a Trailmarker Tree pointing to a ridge that contains an old established trail. Along the ridge can be seen a burl on a tree, twice the size of a basketball. Foresters will tell you a burl is formed naturally when a foreign object is imbedded in the bark, and the bark will grow around the burl to protect the tree. A burl results from a tree undergoing stress due to an injury, virus or fungus, or insect infestation. I have been told from the Ute oral history that the Ute men would often collect kinnikinnick and grasses to dry and smoke as tobacco as part of their prayers. The smoke is drawn through a pipe into the mouth, and as prayers are spoken, it is released through their mouth. When it rises, it carries the prayers to the Creator. The Ute men collect the ashes from the tobacco and carry it in a bag around their neck, as the ashes are sacred. Throughout the winter, as they smoke the ashes are collected. At winter's end the Medicine Man would join all the ashes and select a tree, split bark in the tree and tie on the bag of ashes on the tree in hopes the bag containing the ashes of the prayers would become part of the tree. This too could cause a burl to grow.

Within the private property is found an unusual rock formation that forms a semi-circle, which at one time had a small shelter formed of branches above the formation. The skeleton of the structure has collapsed but is still evident. The rocks in this semi-circle are of different varieties, some of which are not types found in the area. As with all areas in which CMTs are found, it is important to find multiple signs that point to the presence of indigenous people frequenting the area whether it is a tipi ring, fire pits, medicine wheels or petroglyphs. It is our hope that in the future this rock formation and others that we have found near CMTs will be studied by archaeologists to find out more about their origins. Those who have studied CMTs often find the CMT first then look for other signs in the area. Now, when we visit the site with a known stone feature, we look for CMTs too. It is important for future research that stone features that have already been recognized by archaeologists and geologists as belonging to Native Americans be revisited to look for CMTs.

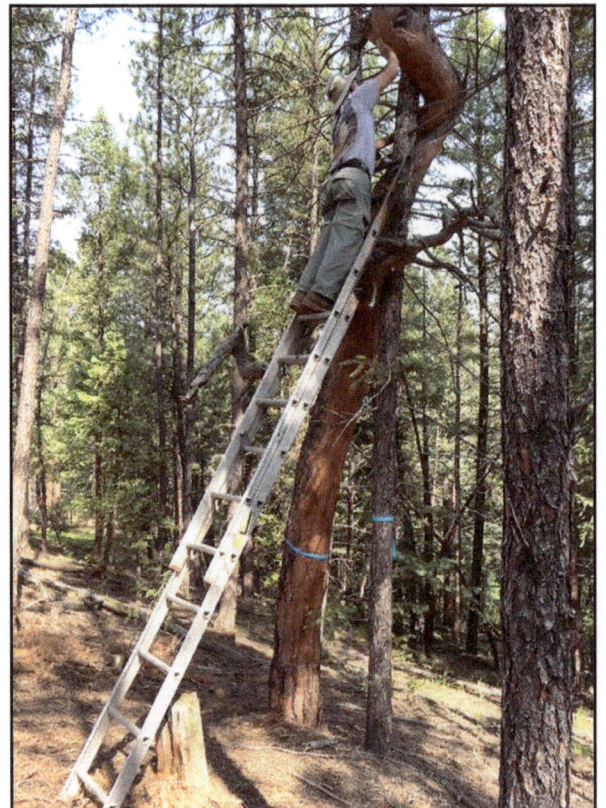

The pictures above show the well extended ladder with forester Bruce Benninghoff looking for ligature marks on the first area where the one tree begins its spiral around the other.

Morrison
Jefferson County

The area around Morrison, Colorado has long been known to the Ute who passed through and camped in the area. Although other Native Americans stayed in the area, the Ute were the most consistent tribe, allowing for multiple visits and extended time needed to modify trees. One of the early ranches, established in 1861 and still owned by the Rooney family, was often visited by the Ute, including Chief Colorow. Chief Colorow (1813-1888) was one of the best known Ute leaders in the 19th century. Although he was born a Comanche, once captured as a child and raised by the Ute, he was considered a Ute. He favored hunting on the Western Slope but would set up camp for weeks in the Evergreen Valley after hunting. His band of Ute would congregate at the Hogback, which became part of Rooney Ranch. The Iron Spring on the Ranch provided a place to bathe and rest after hunting while the women prepared the hides and readied for winter. The grass was plentiful in this area to feed the livestock. Colorow continued to camp in the area annually after the Rooney family started their ranch.

The Ute presence is known by trees that marked trails throughout the area. In the 1800s the Ute held council under a large ponderosa pine that overlooked the ranch on the slopes of Dinosaur Ridge. In 1973, Jefferson County Open Space purchased the acreage containing the "Council Tree" when the National Park Service designated Dinosaur Ridge as a National Natural Landmark. Like many Ute trees, it was called not only by one name, "Council Tree" but was also called the "Inspiration Tree."

Dinosaur Ridge is one of the most famous dinosaur fossil locations. Bones from the Stegosaurus, Apatosaurus, Diplodocus and Allosaurus were found there starting in the late 1800s. In 1937 when a roadway was being constructed, workers found hundreds of dinosaur footprints. Often when there is a rock formation that is of significance, such as a water source, lookout or as in this case, a location of dinosaur prints, CMTs can be found. Dinosaur footprints in Utah also have CMTs nearby.

While in Jefferson County we visited multiple private property locations along the 285 corridor. This route from Santa Fe to Denver was an important trading route for hundreds of years. It comes as no surprise that we found many CMTs, not just the "Council Tree." As we discuss these trees in Jefferson County, we remind you that much of this area is private property and homeowners do not wish for uninvited visitors on their property. However they have consented for us to put photographs of some of these unusual trees in this book. There are many parks, trails and open spaces that also have many CMTs and we ask that you enjoy the CMTs of this area on the designated trails.

Dinosaur footprints found near Morrison, Colorado.

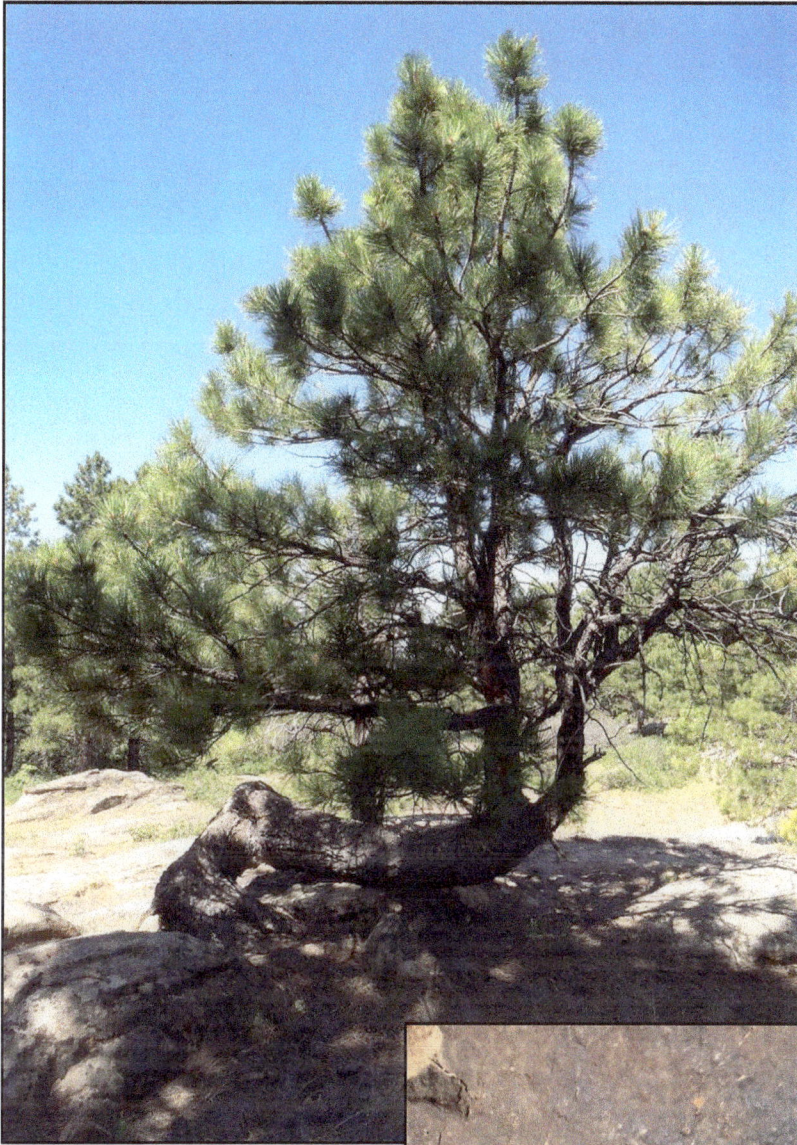

Like the dinosaur prints found in Morrison, the footprints in the photograph at right, found in Utah, are surrounded by CMTs such as the one shown above.

Evergreen
Jefferson County

Carson Louis King was eight months old when his parents moved to Evergreen near Elk Meadows Open Space. For thirteen years he has grown up with two of the most stunning CMTs in his front yard and a fascinating one in his backyard. His father, Louis, is part Cherokee and because of his interest in Native Americans, he named his son Carson, after Kit Carson, a friend to Native Americans. Carson's parents are science teachers and have given him a love of nature. When his father built a tree house for Carson in the back yard, it was built around a tree that has seven branches modified to point in one direction. It is one of the many CMTs found near their property.

When Nicole and Louis purchased the home their realtor told them the two trees in the front yard were Indian trees and pointed to sources of water. It is known there is underground water in the area. There are five to six rows of white rocks that form a half circle around the trees, but when they were placed is unknown. Louis contacted the prior owners of the home and invited them to come to meet with Dr. Jefferson and me to see if any of the many questions regarding the trees and the rocks could be answered. The trees are definitely over two hundred years old. One tree points direct north and the other tree's main trunk points west; it grows under the tree facing north. Then a modification of the second tree forces its trunk to point south. Not even the photograph in the book can do these trees justice. Both trees exhibit the peeled bark pattern known to not only the Ute but also the Cherokee. These two trees, along with other trees attributed to Ute, have the same type of cut. Without a written language from multiple tribes, it is hard to understand if modification practices were shared among tribes. Another interesting point is the trees are shaped somewhat like what the Comanche call their Story Telling Place Tree. The Comanche confirmed one Story Telling Place Tree in Texas, but have found other modified trees in Texas. Although not always peaceful with the Ute, the Comanche and Ute lived in harmony for many years. It would be interesting to know if there was a relationship with these trees and if it could be attributed to Ute, Comanche or both.

Dr. Jefferson said the Comanche and the Ute language are both of the Shoshonean dialect and are derivatives of the ancient Uto-Aztecan language. When the two tribes met they were able to communicate with many of their words being the same. There are references that said the tribes separated in the 1700s. One interesting side note, Dr. Jefferson showed archaeologist Ken Frye a picture of the rocks around these trees. Ken said they are similar to what a Shoshone from the Wind River Reservation in Wyoming told him was a Crescent Moon Healing Circle. The Healing Circle was a place for Medicine Men to hold a ceremony for a person in need of healing. Prayers would be given over a ceremonial fire. Ashes of the fire would be placed around the Crescent Moon shaped rocks. It is unknown when the rocks were placed by these trees; one prior owner said they have been there since the early 1970s when they owned the home, but they were definitely placed by very special trees. If they are a newer addition than when the trees were modified, the persons who placed them might have been familiar with the Crescent Moon Healing Circle. What is known is that young Carson will grow up in the shade of these magnificent trees.

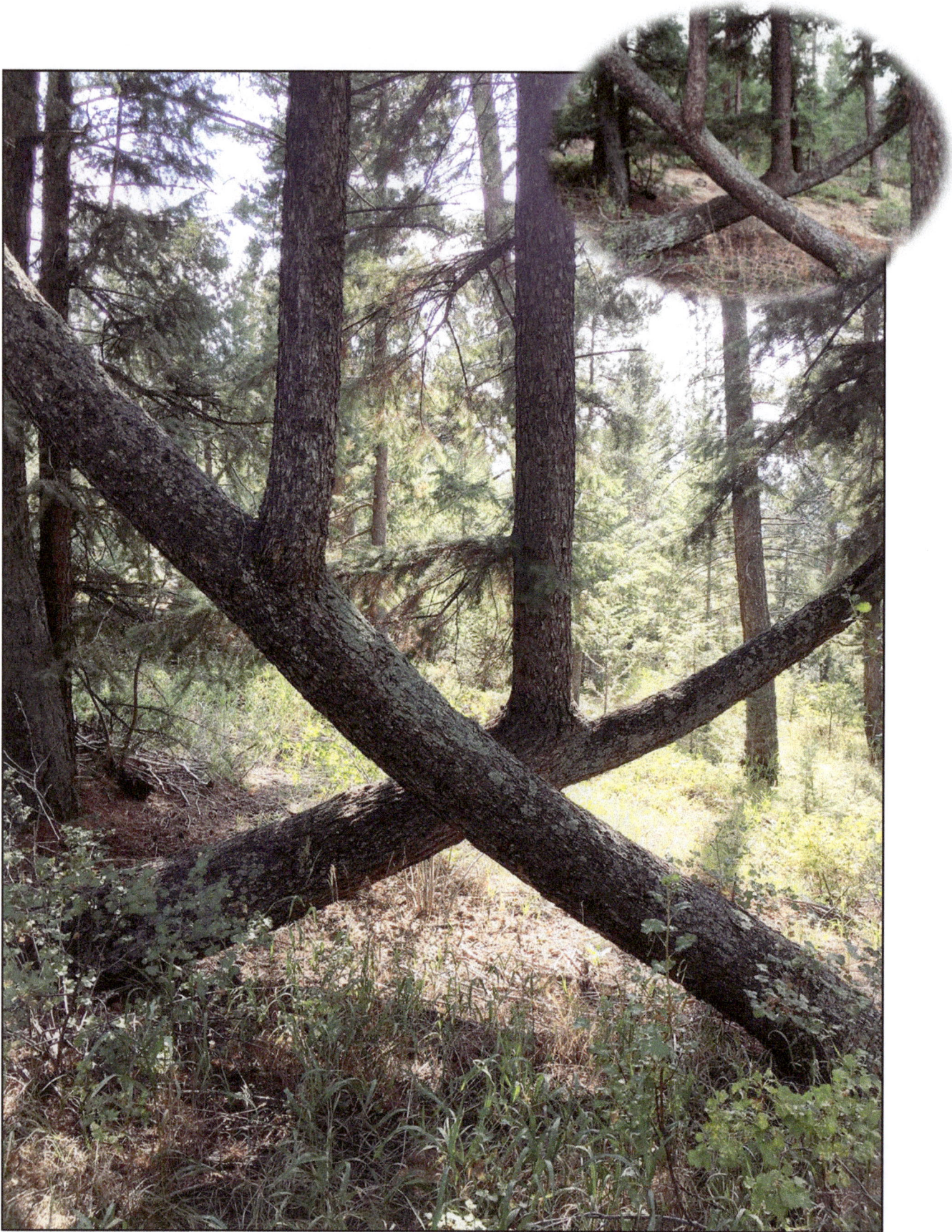

Conifer CMTs pointing to water sources.

Conifer
Jefferson County

Unknown to those who travel west along Highway 285 are several extraordinary CMTs, not along the road but deep within private property. On a narrow trail are two large, old growth trees that have been modified to point in opposite directions, one directly to Kenosha Pass and the other back to the plains. Dr. Jefferson brought to our attention that these trees point to multiple water sources. Near the trees is a flowing spring that leads down to a stone feature. Kenosha Pass is an appropriate name as it is the Native American term for water jug. Forester Bruce Benninghoff has also visited this site. When he saw these trees, he felt in his professional opinion that they could not have been shaped by natural phenomena but were modified by human hands many years ago to specifically be formed in this way. There is no doubt these trees are significant, especially when looked at in the totality of other trees and features in the area.

Another tree in this vicinity is shaped like the window trees found in El Paso County. Near the natural spring is a rocky outcropping surrounded by more CMTs. The outcropping has water basins that could have been naturally formed along the top of the rock. Today they hold snow melt and rain water year round. After visiting during many times of the years, we have observed that these basins always have had water in them. There is evidence of man-made channels or grooves that connect one basin to the next allowing the water in the top basin to flow to the lower basins. Dr. Jefferson stated this filtration system allows sediment to remain in the upper basins. The Ute used this type of filter system knowing that water flowing from one basin to the next becomes purer. Ute women were required to fill two water jugs when going over Kenosha Pass, knowing water can be found on both sides of the pass, but water would need to be carried to have enough to cross over the pass.

The next tree we looked at on this property the owner's daughter said reminded her of a Viking ship. This highly unusual tree grows pointing exactly in the east and west directions. One of the main branches points to the rocky outcropping and the underground spring that bubbles up approximately 100 feet away.

Carl Andrew Koehlers book of 2013 entitled *Talking Trees & Spirit Trails* discusses what he describes as trees shaped like a candelabra or W found in New York State that point to a water source. The trees he has encountered have one main trunk that runs along the ground with three uprights growing out of the main trunk. It was this type of tree, pointing to water, that was the first CMT he encountered. The tree was found in Bull Hill State Forest in an area that the Native Americans called Canacadea, or "where the earth meets the sky."

We also have found trees modified the same way in Teller County, Douglas County and six located in Jefferson County that all point to water sources. As shown on the tree below, the main trunk has been modified to grow along the ground. Where the main trunk has finally been released to grow upward is the direction the tree points to a water source. Large branches have been allowed to grow to form multiple trunks along the original trunk that is on the ground, giving the tree its candelabra shape. Koehler also points out that where there is one CMT there are usually others. He believes the trail trees that mark the path that the indigenous people followed are still talking, relaying the direction to travel. Although the Koehler book discusses CMTs found in the New York State region, they are very similar to those in our area although different species. Once again I will state, as more people study CMTs it will be advantageous to catalogue the similarities found throughout the United States.

Moqui (Moki) Steps
Jefferson County

Janet Shown, the past president of one of the local historical societies in Jefferson County has become a CMT advocate. She has hosted Dr. Jefferson, Bruce Benninghoff and Dr. Lucy Bower when they held CMT awareness training for local residents doing fire mitigation. They instructed private land owners how to tell the difference between natural caused or manmade modification on a tree.

Janet has visited both Ute reservations in Colorado with Dr. Jefferson and me to better understand Colorado's CMTs along with the history and culture of the Ute. She has introduced me to property owners in Jefferson County whose property contains signs of the ancient Ute. One area contained Moqui Steps, arrowheads and CMTs. Moqui is the Ute word for what are commonly spelled Moki.

Moqui Steps are a recurring feature found in the southwest, previously inhabited by ancient Pueblo people and other Native American cultures. A Moqui is a carved feature in a vertical rock that forms a toehold or handhold allowing a person to climb the rock surface to reach a lookout or a dwelling; many are found in Utah and the Mesa Verde area. They are usually two to three inches in depth and three to four inches in height. The Moqui Steps in Jefferson County are on the center of a large boulder. There are handholds each side of the rock feature. The rock is about 18 feet tall and flat on top allowing for a 360 degree view of the area. This would facilitate the Ute or even early settlers looking for game or any approaching enemy. There are several CMTs in close proximity to this rock feature. In the past, bison were known to be in this area.

Although there is no written account of Moqui Steps being carved into trees, circular indentions that have the appearance of being man carved on a CMT found in El Paso County discussed earlier in this book do raise questions about whether these practices were not only done on rocks but also trees. Further study needs to occur in this area.

The area known as Lost Creek Wilderness Area in Jefferson and Park County is sometimes called the last refuge of the American Bison in the United States. In the 1880s a local rancher came upon this area and found the only known herd of wild bison in Colorado, naturally penned in by the surrounding mountains. Upon hearing of the bison a group of Chicago bankers in 1898 formed a hunting party and killed nine. They then turned themselves in to the Justice of the Peace in Leadville and voluntarily paid the fine of $500 per bison, thus being recorded as the last white buffalo hunters in America.

Moqui Steps found on a rock surface in Jefferson County, Colorado.

Pine Ridge
Jefferson County

Another prime example of both Native American stone features and CMTs being discovered within proximity of each other is along an isolated ridge on private property in west Jefferson County. Janet Shown, a local resident, arranged for us to visit a stone feature on property in the area, not knowing if any confirmed CMTs were nearby. The visit allowed us to continue to verify CMTs found near stone features. Studying CMTs and stone features in their original location, known as "in situ," is critical to the interpretation of not only those artifacts, but the history and culture of the people who formed those artifacts and their connection to the land where they were found.

The article "The Medicine Wheels of North America" by Trevor David explains that stone constructions, called medicine wheels, were used by ancient cultures to study the sky, for navigation and spiritual purposes. There are about two hundred medicine wheels in North America. The vast majority of medicine wheels are found in Canada, but some are located in North Dakota, Wyoming, Montana and Colorado. Medicine wheels and tipi rings are considered by some to be endangered as they are subject to theft, vandalism and agriculture. The property in Jefferson County contains one of these stone features, a medicine wheel.

Determining the date range when a rock was place in a stone feature is problematic. One characteristic which helps identify an older site is lichen bridging. Bridging is when the lichen grows from one rock connecting to the next, as shown in the photograph right. This suggests the rocks have been in place long enough for the lichen to grow for several years. There are many CMTs in the area that are in close proximity to the wheel showing the importance of the area. We estimate the

CMTs in this area to be at least two to three hundred years old. At least three CMTs point to the wheel suggesting that the wheel was located on the site first and therefore is older than the modified trees. This also helps establish an approximate date range for when the wheel placement occurred. It is becoming increasingly apparent how important it is to study stone features found in context with CMTs to obtain a more complete understand of the history and culture of the indigenous people.

To validate the Pine Ridge site I wanted to bring a group, all with different degrees and backgrounds, to study the CMTs and rock features in the vicinity: a Ute Elder, an archaeologist, a forester, and other people who have studied CMTs and are familiar with Ute Prayer Trees. When this finally came to fruition, the group, shown in the picture below, contained from left to right: Susie Peterson, Dr. Gary Zigler, Bruce Benninghoff, Jon Moore Koenigsberg, Dr. Lucy Bauer, Janet Shown and Dr. Jefferson.

The general consensus of the group was that the trees were likely attributable to the Ute People and some of the trees were modified after the medicine wheel was created. One of the larger old ponderosa pine Trailmarker Trees pointing to the wheel has a long peeled bark pattern and shows ligature marks. You cannot see the wheel from the tree, it is on the other side of a ridge, but the tree points up over the ridge with the medicine wheel in line on the other side of the ridge. At the top of the ridge is a Douglas fir, one of the oldest trees found on the property, pointing to Pikes Peak. This tree, although pointing to Pikes Peak, is not a Trailmarker Tree but a Story Tree as it has more intricate modifications. The medicine wheel can be seen when looking down the draw from this Douglas fir. Another tree in the area could be an arborglyph. One arborglyph tree in San Juan National Forest shows a man walking; this tree also shows what appear to be the legs of a man walking, in the direction of the wheel.

Archaeologist Dr. Gary Ziegler was among the group of visitors to this site with me on a beautiful October day. He explained that he specialized as an Andean archaeologist with limited knowledge in North American cultures and their ethno history, so he limited his observations to physical and measurable aspects of the site. His description and observations are as follows: "The primary feature is a circular ring of placed, white milky quartz, field stones varying individually in size from several inches to up to two feet across. Two straight lines of stones cross the circle, ninety degrees opposed. They cross at the center meeting a roughly, rectangular-shaped, upright monolith approximately two and one half feet high. The two interior lines are cardinal aligned, north/south and east/west. The circle is situated on top of a small ridge rising within a natural erosional and geological structure formed amphitheater a short distance down below the main ridge crest. An outward focus is southeast toward Pikes Peak. An exposed, fragmented, quartz, pegmatite nearby, serves as a source for the field stones. A number of imported, small, rounded river stones were scattered around. I have seen similar stones at mountain top Andean sites which were left as offerings to the mountain spirits."

"There is an abundant reference to similar shaped features called 'medicine wheels' around North America, see: http://www.atlasobscura.com/articles/the-medicine-wheels-of-North-America."

"The respected archaeologist John Brumley has developed an official definition for the medicine wheel. According to Brumley, a medicine wheel contains at least two of the following three criteria: a central stone cairn, one or more concentric stone circles, two or more stone lines radiating outward from a central point. See: https://archive.org/details/medicinewheelsonbrum."

"The Pine Ridge circle fits all three of his criteria. My first question is always who might of made this and for what purpose. I have seen something similar in other places that were built and used by spiritual seeking, counter-culture groups most frequently in the 1970s." "However, the location on a remote high ridge which had no road or trail access until recently gives low probability to this. Association with other cultural objects; the likely CMTs and a placed stone mound nearby gives a stronger probability to the circle having an earlier, native origin."

"Given the physical evidence and other mentioned consideration, I suggest that the Pine Ridge site is a native "Medicine Wheel" of unknown tribal origin but likely Ute from historical territorial

This Story Tree, in close proximity to a medicine wheel, points to Pikes Peak.

location. The date is undetermined. As always, further study is needed. The use of white quartz gives it a special, unusual and ascetic aspect."

There is also a Burial Tree at this location. Although smaller in stature, it has a very prominent cut at the first bend, where the tree was modified by opening the bark with a sharp instrument and cutting across the fibers to hold the tree down. It has the five major features of a Burial Tree: two 90 degree bends, the orange coloration indicative to age, ligature marks, the horizontal and vertical cuts along the hip and a girdled primary trunk.

Dr. Jefferson visited Jefferson County on many occasions and felt the significance of this site. He came prepared with his sacred tobacco and eagle feather. He feels a great connection to his Ute ancestors at this location and feels energy around this sacred site. The term "medicine" implies that these wheels were sacred to the Native American.

To start our day correctly Dr. Jefferson performed a ceremony with tobacco, smoke and prayer. The unlit tobacco was sprinkled on the ground by the four main stones that mark the four directions. Dr. Jefferson did not interpret the meaning of his prayers or the meaning of the ceremony; it was only for the Ute, but he was gracious to allow us to observe. Dr. Jefferson is 84 years old, and although it is becoming difficult to get around, it was important to him to visit this site, even though it was not an easy hike. Dr. Jefferson teaches that as we visit the forest we should ask permission of the spirits, so the spirits will help guide our learning. He also asked the group to introduce themselves to one another using a Ute tradition of a Talking Stick. The Ute and other Native Americans have used what is called a Talking Stick, which the Elders would designate during a Council. The rules of the Council were that whoever held the stick had the right to talk and all must listen. It is rude to interrupt and one can be expelled from the Council if they talk out of turn.

As we were sharing our thoughts one at a time with the Talking Stick, one beautiful Painted Lady butterfly flew through to the center of the circle of the medicine wheel. Soon a group of the butterflies came down the draw and through the circle. In the fall these butterflies migrate in groups and are often seen together, but the fact they were at this sacred place on the day we visited made it feel special.

Another interesting phenomenon we have observed when traveling with Dr. Jefferson is his relationship with wild animals. On one trip a pair of eagles flew overhead as we walked in the San Juan Mountains. When Dr. Jefferson was busy talking, the group could see the two eagles flying behind him. Trying to get his attention to show him the eagles, Dr. Jefferson said quietly,

"I know they are there." On another trip to the Black Forest for a Ute Prayer Tree retreat a moose visited our group on the opening day. Moose are rarely seen in the area.

I wanted to get a better picture of one of the trees so I returned on another day. When I arrived at the property owner's home, near one of the CMTs and medicine wheel, we saw an animal in motion. It was an inquisitive fox. She watched us and circled the area as we quietly talked. The fox approached us and laid down right by us and took a nap. Then as we walked to the medicine wheel, the fox followed us. It was a very peaceful encounter at such a spiritual site.

Living in Colorado it is common to have encounters with wild animals when in the woods; the deer are abundant. Birds, squirrels and rabbits along with other wildlife live in the mountains. It is during my trips to look at Ute Prayer Trees that I have had encounters, like the ones above, that somehow stand out in my mind as something different, something special. Once when traveling La Veta Pass a wolf came out and slowly crossed the road and made eye contact. Growing up on a ranch, I have seen many coyotes, and this was no coyote. I know that wolves are in New Mexico, and they are not thought to be in Colorado. This was a grey wolf.

Another time traveling through the mountains, I was slowly driving when I noticed a shadow moving to my left side. Looking over I noticed that it was a black bear, traveling parallel to me at a pretty good speed. I slowed down and the bear got ahead of me. He then stopped, turned around and looked at me. Another time when hiking for CMTs, the group I was with was watched by a large male turkey. I am sure that his flock of females was nearby and he was in protection mode, but it was a special sight. Once a group of hiker friends of mine stopped to talk; we were in a circle and in quiet conversation when a hummingbird came to join the circle and stayed hovering for quite some time, right at our eye level. Yes, this is probably just coincidence, but I tend to believe like some of the Native Americans I have come to know, these sights are special and part of the journey of learning what the Creator has given us on Mother Earth. The Ute believe the butterfly, the hummingbird and the eagle are messengers to and from the Creator.

This medicine wheel found in Jefferson County is surrounded by Ute CMTs.

Florissant Fossil Beds
Teller County

One of the most unique Ute Prayer Trees in Teller County has a story as interesting as the tree. Located not far from the Florissant Fossil Beds at what is now called the Barksdale Picnic Area is a beautiful example of a Ute CMT. The tree is very close to an area previously known for its flint, used in arrow making, and sits right off the Shooting Star Trail. It is a large tree that grows over five feet along the ground with three trunks coming out of the main trunk on the ground.

One contact I had found through research was Toby Wells. In 1946 Toby's parents bought a ranch that is now part of the Fossil Beds. Toby grew up on the ranch. For many years the water for their home came from a natural spring nearby. In the early days rocks lined the spring, keeping the growth of weeds at bay. The water flow from this spring at the time was about twenty gallons a minute.

One day when Toby was a young boy in the 1950s, he was out playing on the ranch when a 1949 red Ford pick-up truck pulled up with an older Ute woman and her Ute driver. He got the impression from things she said that she was related to Chipeta and had come down from the Ute reservation in Utah. She told him she was looking for a place where her ancestors mined flint that they would make into arrows to trade with the people of the plains. The woman unrolled a buffalo robe on the top of the hood of the pickup with a map drawn on the inside of the hide of the robe. She pointed to a place on the robe and asked if he knew where a great spring was in the area. Toby showed her the family spring. She then asked where the "indicator tree" to the spring was located. Toby did not know what she was asking, so she told him that the indicator would be a tree that would lead or point to the spring. This is yet another example of different names used, even among the ancient Ute, for CMTs. She pointed out that when coming from gathering the flint along the ridge, if you followed the direction of the trees, you would find the spring. She stated you might still see the depression in the ground where the trail would have been.

Toby knew of one unusual tree nearby that he liked to play on, so he showed her. Then she pointed out the scarring where the tree had been tied to the ground for much of its early growth. Three other tree branches, forming new trunks, grew up from this main truck that had been tied to the ground. When riding on horseback along the ridge, it was easy to spot this tree, thus, easy to find the spring.

Four or five hundred yards from the spring is an open space where there is indication of the encampment where flint was chipped to form arrowheads. This was a perfect place to stay with a clear fresh spring nearby. This tree, with its "W" or candelabra shape is another example of a tree pointing to water, much like the ones found in New York State mentioned in Koehler's book.

CMT pointing to a water source.

Loya's Story
Teller County

The ancestors of today's Ute passed down their history and culture through stories, music, art and ceremonies. Ute Elders still teach this way. One Elder, Loya Arrum, from the Northern Ute Reservation in Utah, told the importance of Ute Prayer Trees. Although Loya has "walked on," the Ute way of saying she passed away, her story will stay alive through the children who heard her. She gave an interview to Don Wells when he was producing the film, "Mystery of the Trees." The Ute don't believe their people who die are gone, their spirits are here. Loya is still telling her story.

For years Loya took children off the reservation to the mountains near Pikes Peak so they could learn about their ancestral lands. She would tell them the Ute were mountain people. She said she cried an ocean for the children that didn't know the mountains or the trees. "The mountains are just beautiful, I think, wow, my ancestors walked on this same trail and I am here, it really touches my soul." She would tell the children "You come from a strong group of people. Your ancestors were so strong because they lived in the mountains." She would explain that most of the trees that are bent by the Ute in Teller County point to Pikes Peak. They were not just for marking trails but were and still are a place to leave an offering to the Creator. Loya used tobacco for her offering as it is a sacred plant. She would tell the children, "We have been told we approach from the west." She went on to teach "We believe that everything is living." She said when she offered a prayer at a Prayer Tree it became part of the tree. The above tree was one of Loya's favorite, pointing to Pikes Peak.

Found near the town of Florissant, Loya called the tree above the Holy Women Tree. She explained her ancestors would bend the tree and the tree would become an Altar. Loya would point out the tree markings where it had been tied down. Loya said when she prays she tells the ancestors that they are loved. "I talk to the spirit of the Prayer Tree; the Prayer Tree is holding the prayers that go to the

Creator." She said she wanted to be honest and only tell the children what the ancestors want to say and share what happened long ago and why they do things in certain ways. "My ancestors need a voice and I feel I am one of the chosen people to speak the truth of our ancestors." It was important to Loya to remember history through songs, dances, ceremonies and stories.

The tree below is a Burial Tree found in Mueller State Park that was visited by Loya and was featured in the film. I had attempted to find the tree with a group of friends in the spring but the snow was too deep and without snowshoes you would sink twelve to eighteen inches.

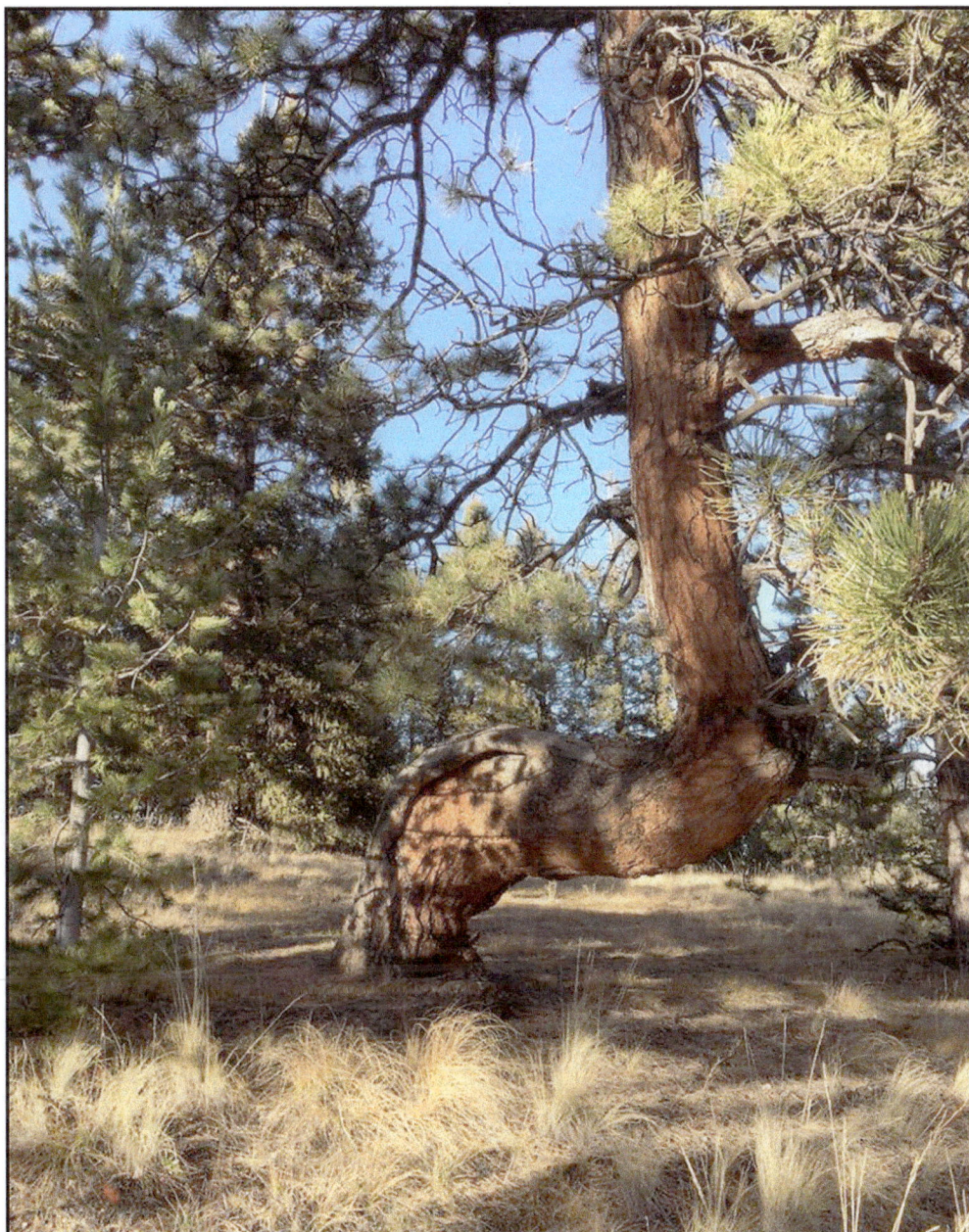

I was determined to find this tree located above 9,000 feet that was so important to Loya's story. On my way home from a visit to the medicine wheel in the fall, I tried again to find the tree before the winter snow would impede me till the following year. After finding the tree, pictured on the previous page, once again I was visited by the last of the Painted Lady butterflies of the season. The butterfly spiraled down like a leaf on its last flights of its life. It landed on the ground at my feet, and when it closed its wings it all but disappeared among the fallen aspen leaves. The butterfly blended into the ground, just like Prayer Trees blend into the forest. It reminded me that my travels exploring CMTs around Colorado began with the collapse of a Prayer Tree in Beulah in the spring and that as winter approached, the life of this butterfly had come full circle, just like the Ute migrated in a full circle in their travels throughout the year in the Shining Mountains. So as the sun was setting over Pikes Peak, the Ute's beloved Tava, I felt this was a good place to end this segment of the incredible journey which I have made with so many friends.

Author's shadow pointing out the end of this stage of his journey as winter approaches.

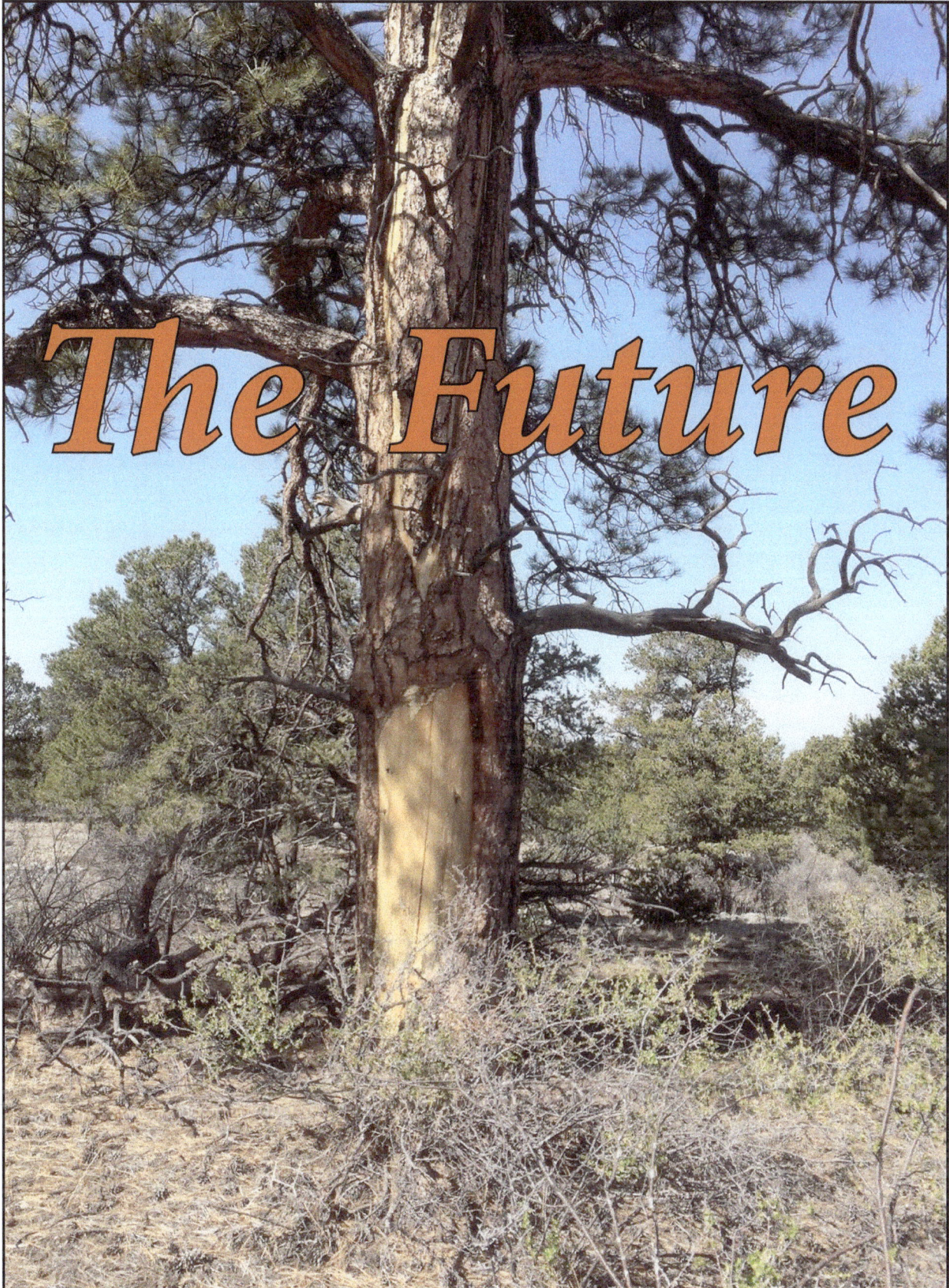

The Future

The Future in Sight

With the culmination of this book I am gratified knowing that many steps forward have occurred toward the protection and documentation of Culturally Modified Trees found in Colorado, joining with many other efforts around the United States and Canada. One milestone along our journey was the launch of a new non-profit organization; the Association for Native American Sacred Trees and Places (NASTaP). The articles of incorporation were filed on the last business day of 2017 for the 501(c) (3) (www.nastap.org). The mission of the non-profit is to inspire discovery, appreciation and conservation of Native American sacred trees and places.

The founding members of NASTaP agreed on the guiding principles: that no one person, tribe, or group has all the answers or knows all the truth. Together; NASTaP can conduct better research, identification, interpretation, documentation, education, and conservation focused on: Culturally Modified Trees (CMTs); modified stones, stacked rocks, and rock art; ceremonial landmarks and landscapes; Native American natural science; and stewardship of the earth, land, water, and sky.

As if a gift from the Creator, donated space unexpectedly became available to headquarter the fledgling non-profit at the historic Glen Isle Resort in Bailey, Colorado. This resort hotel is located on a previous Native American encampment along US Highway 285. New owners of Glen Isle, Mary Ruth and Greg Vincent, purchased the 148 acre property in 2017 and are restoring the grand resort.

Glen Isle was built in 1900 and opened in 1901. For over 90 years it was owned by one family. Mary Ruth vacationed at the resort as a child and once married, continued to come to the resort with her family. When it came up for sale, due to a death in the owner's family, the Vincent family changed their careers and bought the lodge with the desire to make it retain the charm they knew. "We feel we are caretakers of this beautiful place, but it is the community that owns it." Mary Ruth said. They want to be part of the community and sharing their location with NASTaP is one step they have generously made.

Janet Shown, one of my CMT friends mentioned in this book, was intimately familiar with Glen Isle, having worked there many years ago while attending high school and college. Her parents had honeymooned there in the 1950s, and they spent several family vacations at Glen Isle. The main lodge contains many Native American artifacts, and several CMTs have been discovered on the grounds. Janet knew this would be a wonderful location for NASTaP.

Dr. Jefferson decided it would be fitting to dedicate the new NASTaP headquarters at Glen Isle with a traditional Ute blessing. Forty-nine attended the dedication ceremony for the new non-profit, including the Charter Members, and the new Board of Directors. Dr. Jefferson is serving as the President, Janet Shown as Secretary, Mike Vitek as Treasurer, and Kay Van Cleave as Advisory Member. I too, a proud founding member, also attended. Dozens of supporters, family and friends joined hands to form a circle sharing our hopes for the success of this organization. Forty-nine was an appropriate number (7 x 7) as seven is a sacred number to the Ute and other American Indian tribes. Dr. Jefferson once told me that when the Ute were forced onto the reservation it was said it would take seven generations for peace to begin with the white men. The seventh generation has been born and it is hoped this non-profit will help bring different cultures together for a common goal.

Mary Ruth and Greg Vincent and their staff had worked tirelessly to open the lodge and two cabins to host our dedication ceremony. In following Dr. Jefferson's guidance, Greg built a small fire and allowed it to burn down to create a bed of red hot coals. Luke, the youngest boy in attendance, and AJ, the youngest girl, assisted Dr. Jefferson as he rose and approached the fire from the west to place mountain sage on the hot coals as a soft breeze swirled the smoke across the circle.

Dr. Jefferson offered a prayer in Ute, his Native language; then he walked clockwise around the fire ring to sprinkle tobacco as an offering to the four directions: north, east, south and then to the west. At each of the four cardinal directions he stopped and waved his eagle feathers towards the sky. Upon the rising smoke he offered words of prayer to be carried by the smoke to the Creator.

When Dr. Jefferson returned to the west he faced the fire and sang a beautiful Native American song, which he said he had learned as a young man when he worked at the Smithsonian Institute in Washington, D.C. He explained he had not heard the song before until he learned it at the Smithsonian, and he brought the song back with him and sang it many times; now he hears it everywhere he goes throughout Colorado.

Dr. Jefferson shared with us how his people would sing a song during their travels and they had a different song they would sing when traveling in each direction; north, south, east and west. He told us to use all five of our senses when we are exploring the trees - to use our senses of sight, hearing, smell, taste and touch to truly understand the forest. He talked about how everything in the forest is interconnected: the water, rocks, trees, plants, Mother Earth, animals and birds.

Almost on cue two huge black ravens flew overhead and soared playfully, riding the currents on the wind above the river. Greg Vincent later shared that he and Mary Ruth had lived at Glen Isle since last summer. During the ceremony he saw a little white bird land and a rabbit hop out from under one of the cabins. He had not seen either of these two animals before. It was almost as if the land and the forest were coming to life again.

Several participants had commented on the double rainbow that appeared in the rocky canyon to the west of Glen Isle prior to the ceremony. When the ceremony drew to a close, rain drops began to fall softly from the sky. As people made their way inside to look around the lodge or back to their cars to leave for home, a tremendous downpour of heavy cold rain, mixed with some wet snow, fell from the clouds for nearly an hour; completing the promise of spring.

In closing this book, I am reminded of a quote my CMT friend Barry Trester shared with me from Herman Hesse, the German poet, novelist and painter, born in the Black Forest in Germany said, "Trees are sanctuaries. Whoever knows how to speak to them, whoever knows how to listen to them can learn the truth." It is my hope, my friends, you too will come to know CMTs in Colorado and Native American people like the Ute, who with prayer modified these sacred trees.

While there is still much work to be done to preserve these sacred trees and places, I feel good about what we as a team have accomplished thus far on our shared journey of discovery. While I still have many miles to travel on my journey with countless uncertainties in the circle of life, there is one undeniable truth I have come to learn: sacred trees lead to sacred places.

Glossary

The purpose of this glossary is to serve readers as a general guide to help them understand the meaning of a word or term with respect to this book and not to serve as the definitive source for learning about Culturally Modified Trees. Many trees modified by the indigenous people of present-day Colorado may look remarkably similar to trees modified by Native Americans in other areas and may have been modified for a similar purpose (such as way-finding); however, these trees may be referred to differently (e.g., trailmarker tree, thong tree, h-tree, directional tree). Even within the same tribe, such as the Ute, different people may refer to the same tree as a Spirit Tree or a Prayer Tree or may refer to another tree as a Ceremonial Tree or a Prophecy Tree. It would be highly advantageous for the Ute Nation to publish a glossary of terms documenting their cultural tree modification traditions. As Southern Ute Tribal Elder Dr. James Jefferson teaches, "Just because someone learned something one way and another person learned a different way, doesn't make one person right and the other person wrong. They can both be right if they are teaching how they were taught."

Arborglyph – a carving of an image or symbol on the bark of a tree intended to communicate a message (typically a ponderosa pine or aspen tree).

Archaeological site – an area containing physical evidence of past human use or occupation.

Archaeology – the scientific study of historic or prehistoric people and their cultures based on an analysis of their artifacts.

Aspen Carving – an arborglyph carved on the white bark of an Aspen tree (intended to be a short-term message, such as where a camp may have been relocated).

Bedrock Mortar Hole (BRM) –a round depression or hole worn into a rock outcropping or naturally occurring slab of rock used by ancient people for grinding grain, acorns or other food products. Often more than one hole is found in close proximity to another suggesting food grinding was done in groups of people and may have been a social activity often conducted by women of a tribe.

Burial Tree – a tree with two 90º bends to the trunk believed to be pointing to where a person or people were buried or may have died. Some Ute Elders say in their tradition the tree growing up from the ground represents how we all come from Mother Earth. The first 90º bend runs horizontal across the ground representing how all walk across the ground in life: then at the end of life we all ascend to the creator. Most burial trees in Colorado are ponderosa pines; however, Ute Elders do teach how a lone juniper or cedar tree may have been planted by the Medicine Man or Medicine Woman to mark a sacred burial or ceremonial site. A specific burial tree is intended to honor the spirit of one tribal member or members of that person's extended family.

Cambium – the inner layer of bark, which produces a sticky substance rich in nutrients and vitamins (traditionally mixed in hot tea or broth to be used for medicinal or nutritional purposes). Each growing season adds another layer of wood to the tree.

Capote – one of the seven Ute bands - generally inhabited the San Luis Valley near the headwaters of the Rio Grande and the Four Corners area of Colorado, New Mexico, Arizona and Utah.

Ceremonial Tree – a tree that has been modified, planted or transplanted by a Ute Spiritual Leader to mark a site where a sacred ceremony was held (e.g., Bear Dance or Sun Dance).

CMT – Culturally Modified Tree.

Cookie – a cross-section of a tree, usually measuring 1.5-2 inches in width, extracted from the trunk of a tree and used to determine the age of a tree by counting annual growth rings.

Council Tree – a specific tree where Native American people would meet in peace under the shade of the tree to discuss terms (the tree was a well-known or prominent old tree located along a river or trail).

Cross-grain Scarring – horizontal indentations in the bark of a tree running against the natural grain pattern of the bark (evidence of where the tree was tied or staked down during the modification).

Culturally Modified Tree (CMT) – a tree modified by the indigenous people of a region according to their tribal traditions or customs (Culturally Modified Trees in Colorado were used by the indigenous people for navigational, medicinal, educational, burial or ceremonial purposes).

Culture – the complex whole of a society which includes their collective knowledge, beliefs, art, music, ceremonies, traditions and customs.

DBH – Diameter Breast Height, the height where a forester would generally measure, core and document a tree; generally accepted to be about 4.5 feet above ground level (AGL).

Dendrochronology – the science of determining the age of a tree by counting its annual growth rings.

Forester – a person schooled in forestry who is practicing the profession of forestry.

Grand River Ute – one of the seven bands of Ute (also called Parianuc) - once lived along the Grand River in Colorado and Utah.

Growth Rings – the circular rings extending outward from the center of a tree (one ring is typically added for each year of growth).

HAG – Height Above Ground (the distance between the base of the trunk and the bottom of a CMT feature).

Kenosha – woven Native American water jugs.

Ligature – anything that binds or ties (e.g., yucca cordage).

Mano – smooth stones used to grind seeds, meat or plants in food preparation or to make medicine.

Medicine Tree – a tree used for harvesting cambium by extracting the outer bark.

Medicine Wheel – circular stone feature which typically has a central stone cairn, one or more concentric stone circles and two or more rows of rocks extending outward from the central point.

Moqui Steps – (Moki) toeholds or handholds carved into a vertical rock face or tree to help a person climb.

Mouache – one of the seven Ute bands – lived predominately in southern Colorado and northern New Mexico north of Santa Fe and Taos.

Nuche – the name the Ute people referred to themselves as before the Spanish arrived and began to refer to these people as the Yutas (the name later shortened to Utes and then Ute).

Old Growth – a forest defined by well-developed trees and their interdependent ecosystems.

Petroglyph – a carving of an image or symbol into a rock surface (often referred to as Rock Art).

Pictograph – an ancient painting on a rock surface (a form of Rock Art).

Pith Ring – the center growth ring (or Year 1) of a tree.

Prophecy Tree – Intertwined tree that foretells a future event.

Rock Art – human-made ancient marks on natural stone, which include Petroglyphs, marks carved into the rock surface, and Pictographs, which were painted onto the rock surface. Rock art is believed to have been of importance to indigenous peoples across the world who viewed these stone features as sacred.

Story Tree – A tree that was modified or shaped to communicate a story or convey a message.

Tabeguache – (also known as the Uncompahgre) were the largest of the seven Ute bands and previously lived from the Uncompahgre River eastward across the Rockies to the Front Range (the Tabeguache are also referred to as the "People of Sun Mountain" – Sun Mountain is today known as Pikes Peak).

Tipi – (teepee) a cone-shaped tent, traditionally made of animal hides wrapped around a wooden structure made of lodge poles (the Ute tipi was typically constructed by using 13 –15 lodge poles measuring 12 –14 feet in length; each lodge pole had a position, specific name and virtue often taught by the women to the children during tipi construction).

Trailmarker Tree – a tree bent for navigational purposes to mark a trail (used in way-finding); a Ute Trailmarker Tree traditionally has one 30 degree bend to the trunk and is usually ponderosa pine or Douglas fir; however, as Dr. Jefferson teaches, "We used whatever Creator provided."

Uintah Ute – one of the seven bands of Ute - previously inhabited the Uintah Basin of western Colorado and eastern Utah.

Ute – recognized as the indigenous Native American people of present-day Colorado.

Weeminuche – one of the seven Ute bands - occupied the valley along the San Juan River and its tributaries in northwestern New Mexico and southern Colorado.

Yampa – one of the seven Ute bands - once inhabited the Yampa River Valley and adjacent lands.

Yutas – the name given to the native people who lived in the mountains north of Santa Fe and Taos by the early Spanish explores (the letters "Y" and "s" were eventually dropped; the state of Utah was named in honor of the Ute People).

Bibliography

1. **Anderson, John Wesley.** *Ute Indian Prayer Trees of the Pikes Peak Region*, Old Colorado City Historical Society, Colorado Springs, CO 2015

2. **Becker, Cynthia S., and Smith, David P.** *Chipeta: Queen of the Utes*, A Biography, Western Reflections Publishing Company, Lake City, CO 2006

3. **Borowsky, Larry.** *The Ute Indian Museum, A Capsule History and Guide*, History Colorado, The Colorado Historical Society, Greeley, Colorado 2009

4. **Broome, Jeff.** *Cheyenne War: Indian Raids on the Roads to Denver 1864-1869*, Aberdeen Books, Sheridan, Colorado 2013

5. **Broome, Jeff.** *Dog Soldier Justice: The Ordeal of Susanna Alderdice in the Kansas Indian War*, University of Nebraska Press, Lincoln, Nebraska 2003

6. **Butler, William B.** *The Fur Trade in Colorado*, Western Reflections Publishing Company, Lake City, CO 2012

7. **Carson, Phil.** *Across the Northern Frontier: Spanish Explorations in Colorado*. Johnson Books, Boulder, Colorado 1998

8. **David, Trevor.** *The Medicine Wheels of North America*, Atlas Obscura, 2010

9. **Decker, Peter R.** *The Utes Must Go! American Expansion and the Removal of a People*, Fulcrum Publishing, Golden, Colorado, 2004

10. **Eaton, Rachel Caroline.** *John Ross and the Cherokee Indians, Native American Leaders*, BiblioLife Antiquarian eBooks, Curating History, The Collegiate Press, George Banta Publishing Company, Menasha, Wisconsin 1914

11. **FitzPatrick, Val.** *Red Twiligh: The Last Free Days of the Ute Indians*, Yellow Cat Publishing, Yellow Cat Flats, UT 2000

12. **Goodson, Gary Sr.** *Slaghts/Granit Vale/ Fairville/Shawnee, Colorado Historical Sketches 1859-2013, Book V*, Gary Goodson, Shawnee, Colorado, 2008

13. **Gray-Kanatiiosh, Barbara A.** *Ute, Native Americans (Series)*, Checkerboard Social Studies (Children's) Library, ABDO Publishing Company, Edina, MN 2004

14. **Gulliford, Andrew.** *Sacred Objects and Sacred Places, Preserving Tribal Traditions*, The University Press of Colorado, Boulder, CO 2000

15. **Gwynne, S.C.** *Empire of the Summer Moon: Quanah Parker and the Rise and Fall of the Comanche*, the Most Powerful Tribe in American History, Scribner, New York, NY 2014

16. **Herrera, Carlos R.** *Juan Bautista de Anza: The King's Governor in New Mexico*, University of Oklahoma Press, Norman, OK 2015

17. **Hill, Don**. *Listening to Stone:, Learning in Leroy Little Bear's Laboratory: Dialogue in the World Outside*, Alberta Views, September 2018

18. **Howbert, Irving**. *Memories of a Lifetime in the Pike's Peak Region*, Morris Publishing, Nebraska 1925 (reprinted with permission, Old Colorado City Historical Society, 2007)

19. **Howbert, Irving**. *The Indians of the Pike's Peak Region*, The Rio Grande Press, Inc., Glorieta, New Mexico 1914

20. **Jefferson, James M., Delaney, Robert W. & Thompson, Gregory C**. *The Southern Utes: A Tribal History*, Southern Ute Tribe, Ignacio, Colorado 1973

21. **Jefferson, James**. *Trail Trees Along the Old Spanish Trail*, The Southern Ute Drum, 2016

22. **Kessler, Ronald E**. *Anza's 1779 Comanche Campaign*, 2nd Edition, Adobe Village Press, Monte Vista, CO 2001

23. **Koehler, Carl Andrew**. *Talking Trees & Spirit Trails*, Treeling Books, Avoca, NY 2013

24. **Litvak, Dianna**. *El Pueblo History Museum, A Capsule History and Guide*, Colorado Historical Society, Denver, CO 2006

25. **Mann, Charles C**. *1491: New Revelations of the Americas Before Columbus*, Vintage eBooks, Random House, Inc., New York, 201$_1$

26. **Marsh, Charles S**. *People of the Shining Mountains: The Utes of Colorado*, Pruett Publishing Company, Boulder, CO 1991

27. **Mathews, Carl F. and Matthews, E.C**. *Early Days Around the Divide*, Sign Book Company, St. Louis, MO 1969

28. **Martin, Curtis**. *Ephemeral Bount: Wickiups, Trade Goods, and the Final Years of the Autonomous Ute*, The University of Utah Press, Salt Lake City, UT 2016

29. **Martinez, Wilfred O**. *Anza and Cuerno Verde: Decisive Battle*, Second Edition, Mother's House Publishing, Colorado Springs, CO 2004

30. **McConnell Simmons, Virginia**. *The Ute Indians of Utah, Colorado, and New Mexico*, Published by the University Press of Colorado, Boulder, CO 2000

31. **Michno, Gregory F**. *Encyclopedia of Indian Wars: Western Battles and Skirmishes, 1850-1890*, Mountain Press Publishing Company, Missoula, MT 2003

32. **O'Brien, Greg**. *Chronology of Native Americans: The Ultimate Guide to North America's Indigenous Peoples*, Metro Books, New York, NY 2011

33. **Page, Jake**. *In the Hands of the Great Spirit: the 20,000-Year History of American Indians*, Free Press, Simon & Schuster, Inc., New York, NY 2003

34. **Pettit, Jan**. *Ute: The Mountain People*, Johnson Books, Boulder, CO 2012

35. **Pierson, Francis J**. *Summit of Destiny: Taming the Pikes Peak Country 1858-1918*, Charlotte Square Press, Denver, CO 2008

36. **Rockwell, Wilson**. *The Utes a Forgotten People*, Western Reflections Publishing Company, Montrose, CO 2006

37. **Santoro, Nicholas J**. *Atlas of the Indian Tribes of North America and The Clash of Cultures*, University, Inc., Bloomington, New York, 2009

38. **Saunt, Claudio**. *West of the Revolution: An Uncommon History of 1776*, W.W. Norton & Company, London 2014

39. **Sides, Hampton**. *Blood and Thunder: An Epic of the American West*, Anchor Books (eBooks), Random House, LLC., Knopf Doubleday Publishing Group, 2006

40. **Simmons, Beth, PhD**. *Colorow! A Colorado Photographic Chronicle*, published by the Jefferson County Historical Commission and Friends of Dinosaur Ridge, Morrison, CO 2015

41. **Smith, Anne M**. *Ute Tales,* Volume 29 of the University of Utah, Publications in the American West, University of Utah Press, Salt Lake City, UT 1992

42. **Smith, David P**. *Ouray, Chief of the Utes: The Fascinating Story of Colorado's Most Famous and Controversial Indian Chief*, Wayfinder Press, Ridgeway, CO 1990

43. **Sprague, Marshall**. *Newport in the Rockies*, Swallow Press, Ohio University Press, Athens, Ohio, Fourth Edition, 1987

44. **Stanford, Dennis J. and Day, Jane S**. *Ice Age Hunters of the Rockies*, Denver Museum of Natural History and University Press of Colorado, P.O. Box 849, Niwot, CO 1992

45. **St. Clair Robson, Lucia**. *Ride the Wind: The Story of Cynthia Ann Parker and the Last Days of the Comanche*, Ballantine Books, Random House, New York, NY 1982

46. **Sun Bear, Wabun Wind and Crysalis Mulligan**. *Dancing with the Wheel: The Medicine Wheel Workbook*, A Sun Bear Book, A Fireside Book, Published by Simon & Schuster, New York, NY 1991

47. **Sweeten-Shults, Lana**. *Making its Mark: Comanche Nation to Recognize Indian Marker Tree*, Times Record News, 2017

48. **Taylor, Morris F**. *Ka-Ni-Ache*, The Colorado Magazine, XLIII/4 1966

49. **Thomas, Alfred Barnaby**. *Forgotten Frontiers, A Study of the Spanish Indian Policy of Don Juan Bautista de Anza, Governor of New Mexico 1777-1787, From the Original Documents in the Archives of Spain, Mexico, and New Mexico*, University of Oklahoma Press, Second Printing, Norman, OK 1969

50. **Ubbelohde, Carl & Benson, Maxine & Smith, Duane A**. *A Colorado History* (8th Edition), Pruett

Publishing Company, Boulder, Colorado 2001

51. **Utley, Robert M**. *The Story of the West: A History of the American West and Its People*, DK Publishing Inc., New York, New York, 2003

52. **Virga, Vincent and Grace, Stephen**. *Colorado: Mapping the Centennial State Through History: Rare and Unusual Maps from the Library of Congress*, the Morris Book Publishing, LLC., Guilford, CT 2010

53. **Von Ahlefeldt, Judy**. *Thunder, Sun and Snow: A History of Colorado's Black Forest*, Century One Press, Colorado Springs, Colorado 1979

54. **Waters, Frank**. *Book of the Hopi*, Penguin Books, New York, NY 1972

55. **West, Elliott**. *The Contested Plains: Indians, Goldseekers, and the Rush to Colorado*, University Press of Kansas, Lawrence, Kansas, 1998

56. **Whiteley, Lee**. *The Cherokee Trail, Bent's Old Fort to Fort Bridger*, The 1999 Merrill Mattes Brand Book, Volume XXXIII, Published by the Denver Posse of Westerners, Inc., Johnson Printing, Boulder, CO 1999

57. **Wismer, David A. and Wright, Gary T**. *Shamrock Ranch: Celebrating Life in Colorado's Pikes Peak Country*. Johnson Books, Boulder, Colorado 2009

58. **Wood, Nancy**. *War Cry on a Prayer Feather*, Doubleday & Company, Inc., Garden City, NY 1979

59. **Wood, Nancy**. *When Buffalo Free the Mountains: The Survival of America's Ute Indians*, Doubleday & Company, Inc., Garden City, NY 1980

60. **Wroth, William**. *Ute Indian Arts & Culture: From Prehistory to the New Millennium*, Published by the Taylor Museum of the Colorado Springs Fine Arts Center, 2000

61. www. atlasobscura.com/articles/the-medicine-wheels-of-north-america

62. www.coloradoencyclopedia.org

63. www.trueviralnews.com

64. www.manataka.org

65. www.mountainstewards.org

66. www.nps.gov, **Culturally Modified Trees**, Florissant Fossil Beds, 2017

67. www.sfiprogram.org

The Author

John Wesley Anderson has lived in the Pikes Peak Region since 1956 and grew up in the shadow of Pikes Peak on a ranch in eastern El Paso County where he loved riding horses and collecting arrowheads. John enjoyed a thirty-year law enforcement career with the Colorado Springs Police Department and two four-year terms as the elected Sheriff for El Paso County. John retired from law enforcement and went to work for defense contractor Lockheed Martin. John now pursues his love of history and writing.

While conducting field research for his first book, *Ute Indian Prayer Trees of the Pikes Peak Region*, and his second book, *Native American Prayer Trees of Colorado*, John has driven over 2,500 miles, visited more than half the 64 counties in Colorado and confirmed the existence of many Culturally Modified Trees (CMTs). John has made multiple trips to the Southern Ute, the Ute Mountain Ute and the Northern Ute Reservations. All but one of those visits was in the company of one or more Ute Elders.

Much of John's academic and field research, both on and off the Reservations, was conducted along with professional foresters, archaeologists, anthropologists, botanists, educators and ecologists, many of whom held doctorate degrees in their respective fields of study. John has given more than 164 talks and hikes across Colorado to help spread awareness about these living Native American artifacts.

To study the history and culture of the indigenous people of Colorado, John researched extensive collections of arrowheads, mano, metate, pottery, baskets and Native American artifacts and photographs in private and public collections, including the Pioneers Museum in Colorado Springs, Colorado, Ute Pass Historical Society Museum in Woodland Park, Colorado, Denver Museum of Nature and Science in Denver, Colorado and the Native American Museum in Washington, D.C.

Another of John's books, *Rankin Scott Kelly, First Sheriff El Paso County, Colorado Territory (1861-1867)*, also published by the Old Colorado City Historical Society, received a 2017 Literary Award from the Colorado Springs Historical Preservation Alliance.

www.ingramcontent.com/pod-product-compliance
Lightning Source LLC
Chambersburg PA
CBHW062009150426
42812CB00013BA/2586